Finding Gracie

Finding Gracie

Grace Sanchez

Copyright © 2019 by Grace Sanchez

Editors: C. Flanagan & T. Bergstrom

Love Wins Publishing
Redlands, California

All rights reserved. This book or any portion thereof may not be reproduced or used in any manner whatsoever without the express written permission of the publisher except for the use of brief quotations in a book review.

Printed in the United States of America

First Printing, 2019

"The only impossible journey is the one you never begin."
Tony Robbins

Table of Contents

Introduction..9
Day 1: Working Out a Way to Love Yourself........................13
Day 2: The Gift of Solitude...17
Day 3: Spring Cleaning..21
Day 4: The Magic of Gratitude..25
Day 5: Struggle and Surrender..29
Day 6: The Forgiveness Factor..33
Day 7: Walking the Camino Pt 1..37
Day 8: Walking the Camino Pt 2..41
Day 9: Walking the Camino Pt 3..45
Day 10: Walking the Camino Pt 4......................................49
Day 11: Why I Started My Own Business Pt 1......................53
Day 12: Why I Started My Own Business Pt 2......................57
Day 13: The Beauty of Transitions Pt 1..............................61
Day 14: The Beauty of Transitions Pt 2..............................65
Day 15: The Sanchez Family Pt 1......................................69
Day 16: The Sanchez Family Pt 2......................................73
Day 17: The Sanchez Family Pt 3......................................77
Day 18: The Power of Hope...81
Day 19: Launching My New Life Pt 1.................................85
Day 20: Launching My New Life Pt 2.................................89
Day 21: Gracie's Secret Pt 1..93
Day 22: Gracie's Secret Pt 2..97
Day 23: Gracie's Secret Pt 3..99
Day 24: The Importance of Being Mindful.........................105

Day 25: The Covenant of Friendship.......................................109
Day 26: The Key to My Happiness...................................113
Day 27: You Can't Buy Happiness...................................117
Day 28: Opening My Home, Sharing My Life......................121
Day 29: Balancing Work, Life, and Family Pt 1....................125
Day 30: Balancing Work, Life, and Family Pt 2....................129
Day 31: Balancing Work, Life, and Family Pt 3....................133
Day 32: Embracing the Season of Gratitude.........................137
Day 33: When Relationships Are Complicated Pt 1.................141
Day 34: When Relationships Are Complicated Pt 2.................145
Day 35: Some Encouragement if You've Had a Tough Year......149
Day 36: The Importance of Kindness................................153
Day 37: The Holiday Traditions.......................................157
Day 38: How to Be a Blessing to Others This Holiday.............161
Day 39: When it Feels Like No One's Noticing You................165
Day 40: Rejoice, Don't Resolve.......................................169
Bonus: Forgiving Yourself When Dreams Don't Come True.......173

Introduction

Both my parents were from Mexico and I have a deep love for my culture. My birth name was Graciela Sanchez. In Spanish, *"dar gracias"* means "to give thanks." My parents gave me the name *Graciela* as an expression of gratitude to God for my life. We primarily spoke Spanish at home, but my parents wanted me to feel comfortable with my name as I started kindergarten. So they called me "Gracie." "Gracie" means love and gratitude. I've always felt that the name represents a childlike way of living, of believing the best of others, of being quick to forgive and abundant in love.

I always liked my name and felt that it fit me, if that makes any sense. As a little girl, I was funny, lighthearted and very friendly. I remember my teachers always complimenting my helpful attitude and some would say that I was named appropriately. I have always enjoyed speaking Spanish, and when I was younger, I loved introducing myself as Graciela Sanchez. But one day, I made a fateful decision that would shift my identity forever.

I remember that day as if it was yesterday. It was my sixteenth birthday, May 18th. As I was getting ready for my mother to drive me to the DMV, I told her that I was going to change my name to Grace instead of Gracie. I'll never forget the look on her face as she asked me, *"Mija*, why would you do that?"

My response surprised her. I told her, "Mom, there's no Princess *Gracie*, but there is a Princess *Grace*." Little did I know that on this day, at the young age of 16, I was beginning a life of focusing on my image and constantly striving. I often wonder if my childhood history of sexual abuse played into my decision to leave behind the secret that I carried. I was absolutely convinced that no one would ever dare question a successful girl named Grace.

Throughout high school, I got involved in everything I could possibly get involved in. I served in student government, I belonged to various clubs, and I enjoyed being a cheerleader. I was a straight-A student with big dreams of success. And with a name like Grace, I felt I could somehow achieve my dreams and leave behind that hurt little girl, Gracie.

As strange as it sounds, I had subconsciously hidden that little girl, Gracie, from my life all those years ago. To me, she had come to represent weakness and pain. So I pushed her into a closet and seldom allowed her to come out and play.

As I grew older, I went off to college, and the name Grace gave me the confidence and strength I had longed for. I became very driven and worked hard to gain an edge which would fit the image I was chasing. Little did I know that I was losing myself in the process. I was drifting further and further away from who God created me to be: Gracie.

Then, in 2009, I experienced a life-changing event that I often refer to as my "earthquake." I often joke that not only was it an earthquake, but it was followed by a tsunami. Little did I know that this dark season in my life would lead me on a journey of personal growth and self-discovery. While I started to draw closer to God and leaned into the pain of my situation, I began to see glimpses of my inner child, Gracie. As time passed, I began to simplify my life by purging myself of material things and relationships that were no longer consistent with the woman I was becoming.

Along the way, I discovered that I enjoyed drinking root beer, riding bikes and just being silly. I began to enjoy living in the moment. I learned to be still and trust the process of life. I was shedding the overly serious, intense person that I had become all those years ago. I felt a great relief when I no longer had to pretend to be someone I wasn't. At last, Gracie was returning.

After many years of therapy, I finally made peace with myself and sought my own forgiveness. I bought a doll that resembled me as a child, a little Gracie. I promised her that I wouldn't ever allow anyone to hurt or abuse her again. I learned to compliment little Gracie, to embrace and celebrate her gifts and talents.

One day, I experienced a moment of clarity when I realized that this painful event had brought me to a new truth about myself. That truth became a blessing. My desire to share my life lessons and words of hope to inspire others is the driving force behind Finding Gracie.

I learned self-love by speaking positivity and love to myself. Not only did I bring Gracie out of the closet where I had hidden her long ago, but I gave her free rein over my life. I was truly lost, and now I'm found. And I want to help others reach that same feeling of freedom and forgiveness.

Grace Sanchez

Working Out A Way To Love Yourself

My daily workout routine seems like nothing special, but it is very special to me. It's taken a while to get there. You see, I always associated working out with losing weight or dieting. For years I was hot and cold. I would often start new diets and begin new workout routines. I must have done this cycle for 20 years.

It took me so long to figure out that I had a hard time truly loving others because I didn't know how to love myself. Not being able to love myself partially explains why I was always yo-yo dieting and seeking the latest workout fad. But those diets and workouts also hid a very real fear. I was afraid to love myself, and that fear held back my potential.

So after years of starving myself on diets, I gave in. I decided to love myself for who I was. I decided to cancel all of my gym memberships except for one. I decided to treat my body with the love I would expect from someone else. I drank root beer when I wanted it. Sometimes I ate a burger for lunch instead of a salad. I began working out just to have fun and to relieve stress. And you know what? I lost weight. I enjoyed working out. I fell in love with my closest friends and family. I became a new person capable of *loving without fear*.

Almost every worldview has a variation of the Golden Rule. *The Mahabharata*, a Hindu text, says it like this: "This is the sum of duty; do naught onto others what you would not have them do unto you." In the Sunnah, one of the sacred books of Islam, the prophet Muhammad says, "No one of you is a believer until he desires for his brother that which he desires for himself." And in the Christian Bible, Jesus says, "Love the Lord your God with all your heart and with all your soul and with all your mind. This is the first and greatest commandment. And the second is like it: Love your neighbor as yourself." I think we often overlook the last part.

If we are instructed to love others as we love ourselves, doesn't that mean we have to know how to love ourselves first? For many people, the thought of loving yourself seems like vanity or selfishness. So if we don't love ourselves, can we love others properly either? As we dive into knowing ourselves and being able to love ourselves, we will learn how to better love others.

If you find yourself caught in the same trap I was in, there is hope. Our society calls doing things for yourself selfish and negative. Resist that false idea. Believe that you can enjoy things in your life without feeling guilty. *Trust that loving without fear is possible.* If you do this, you will be able to love others more because you've shown yourself love first.

My Thoughts & Notes

_____

_____

_____

_____

_____

_____

_____

_____

_____

_____

The Gift of Solitude

Solitude is almost a foreign concept today. We're connected to other people 24 hours a day. Most of us sleep with smartphones inches from our head. We stare at computer monitors for hours at a time at work and call watching television while checking social media "unwinding." We've completely lost the ability to be alone.

Almost every worldview strongly encourages meditation for personal and spiritual growth. The Buddha is believed to have found enlightenment from searching within. A famous Psalm, "Be still and know that I am God," has been a meditation mantra for rabbis and priests for hundreds of years. So, what can we learn about ourselves in a time of solitude? The answer: *much more than you think.*

For years, I associated doing nothing with laziness. But really, I was scared of what I might find inside myself if I stayed still. So I buried myself in work and planning. I did whatever I could think of to avoid being alone. That pattern led to a collapse that left me with almost nothing. I finally built up enough courage to be still. What I found was a gift I never knew I had.

I spent time at a lake in southern California, sitting on the beach, listening to the wind run through the trees and the small waves lap gently on the beach. I didn't have an iPod, a book, a cell phone or even a watch. I just sat there. I didn't pray. I didn't talk to myself. *I was, well, still.* Minutes passed like seconds and hours like minutes.

I had never experienced such spiritual rejuvenation. I could sit there in bliss for hours. It was during an afternoon in solitude that I had a vision of myself painting a mural. I hadn't touched a paintbrush since the 2nd grade, so I was very confused by this vision. Later that week, I enrolled in painting classes and discovered a talent I never knew I had.

Now, I paint every couple of weeks and make time to be by myself. As often as possible, I try to get to the lake where it all started. Sometimes I enjoy a whole afternoon in solitude, sometimes just a half hour. I have to schedule my time alone wherever I may be.

I've developed 5 techniques that might help you find the solitude you need and deserve!

5 Techniques to Find the Gift of Solitude

1. *Put it in your calendar.*

I treat my solitude sessions like I'm meeting an important client. Give the session an important-sounding name in your calendar. This helps if someone asks you to do something during that time. Otherwise you might come up with an excuse to blow it off.

2. *Ask someone to hold you accountable.*

This technique might help you follow through if you don't like letting people down. Give it a try. Just make sure you don't invite that person to join you. That would defeat the purpose!

3. *Unplug and power down*

If you can't make the time to get away or get outside, have your solitude time at home. Turn off your cell phone, power down your computers, unplug the TV. Find a spot in your house or backyard and just be still. Listen to what's around you. Just remember to turn everything back on when you're done!

4. *Long drives are your friend*

Living in southern California, I spend a lot of time in my car. Turning off the radio and phone can turn a stressful car ride into meaningful solitude. Be safe, though—don't try this technique when you're tired.

5. *Write*

Take some time to set down your thoughts after your solitude session. You'll find a refreshed and renewed perspective on just about everything. When you look back at these writings later, you may be shocked at what you discovered about yourself.

My Thoughts & Notes

Spring Cleaning

Whoever first invented spring cleaning must have been really tired of winter. We don't get much winter weather here in Southern California. But once the days get longer and brighter, I start thinking about how I can improve my space. Although I live pretty simply now, it took me a long time to figure out how to keep only the few things that bring me joy.

Chances are you've got a lot of stuff around the house that you don't really need or use, but that's still in pretty good shape. Spring is as good a time as any to clear it all away, organize your home, and maybe make a few dollars to boot. You don't have to do everything all at once; focus on one area at a time. Breaking up the tasks into smaller chunks will help you to manage the job so that you won't feel overwhelmed.

More importantly, helping to arrange and organize your personal space can help you to feel refreshed and renewed. I always feel relief when I've finally decided to let go of something I've been keeping around that I don't need any more. Whether it's a skirt that I bought and never wore or a set of mystery books that have been gathering dust since I read them last year, passing them on to someone else can be very freeing.

When we have a lot of clutter in our house—or in our mind—that can make it difficult to focus. Holding on to old clothes and shoes can keep us from enjoying our home and really knowing what we have to wear. In much the same way, holding on to old thoughts and ideas can keep us from enjoying our days and really knowing what we can do.

So while I put my personal space in order, I like to work on putting my internal space in order as well. Thinking about what I'm grateful for and what's important to me helps me to feel happier and more grounded. And that helps me to be more intentional about what I put in my closet—as well as what thoughts I put in my mind.

What are some things that you can let go of this spring? Are there old hurts and worries that you're keeping close to your heart? As you look around your home this spring and think about how much you actually need, look inside too, and see what you can let go of this year.

My Thoughts & Notes

_____

_____

_____

_____

_____

_____

_____

_____

_____

_____

_____

_____

_____

_____

_____

_____

_____

The Magic of Gratitude

It's easy to be grateful when we get things that we want. If someone gives us a beautiful gift or cooks us a delicious meal, it's natural to smile and to thank them and to feel real gratitude. But what about when the things we get aren't what we asked for, or even something we actively dread? Can we find the strength to be grateful for things we get that we never asked for?

Sometimes it's really easy to get caught up in all the things we don't have, all the things we wish we had. When my marriage fell apart, I felt lost and unloved. I felt angry and hurt and defeated. And I can tell you that gratitude was definitely not a feeling it even occurred to me that I could feel again.

But I had children who needed me, and I had friends and family who rallied around me and loved me when I didn't feel that I could love myself. And they helped me recover my joy, my peace, and most importantly, my feeling of gratitude. I learned to be grateful for my friends' love and support, for my children and their needs, and even for my own pressing need to get to work and sort out all the loose ends that a divorce leaves behind.

I will forever be grateful for the way my friends and family brought me back to myself. I can even be grateful, now, for the end of my marriage and the fullness of the life that recovering from it brought me.

Our obligations to ourselves and to each other and our society can too often feel like a burden, but they really are a gift. Without those ties that bind us together, nothing would work. Without the love and labor of thousands of people you'll never meet, you wouldn't have the sandwich you ate for lunch yesterday, or the car you drive, or the clothes you wear. Take a moment, right now, wherever you are, to thank them, to feel the magic of gratitude. And remember that the work you do helps others that you'll never meet.

Are there ten things you can think of to feel grateful about today? If that seems like too many, how about five? Sometimes, all you need is one tiny spark—one memory of flowers or the smell of fresh bread or an old song unexpectedly heard in a shop or out the window of a car, to light a warming fire of gratitude.

While it's true that there aren't any easy answers in life, letting ourselves feel real, unfiltered gratitude is the closest thing to magic I know. Open yourself to gratitude today and let it warm your heart and lift your spirit.

My Thoughts & Notes

_____

_____

_____

_____

_____

_____

_____

_____

_____

_____

_____

_____

_____

Struggle and Surrender

I've never been much of an equestrian, but I admire the artistry and skill displayed by horses and riders. I'm fascinated by the way that the large, powerful horse submits to its rider. And the rider must earn that respect and submission through persistent, faithful training. This blend of talent, nature and skill pushes both man and horse to new limits.

Imagine a beautiful mustang running wild and free in an open field, enjoying the freedom we all dream of. Sometimes, he feeds from a rancher's trough and slips away before the rancher can touch him.

Is it the struggle that matters, or what we become as we engage in it?

The rancher knows the wild mustang well, and he respects the beautiful creature. This morning, the mustang is hungry and feeds from the rancher's trough. Tomorrow, maybe he'll stay.

Time passes, and the mustang gets stronger and wiser. He visits the ranch often and enjoys the company of the other horses on the ranch. He watches from a safe distance as the rancher trains the other horses.

One morning, the rancher finds the wild mustang running around in the corral. Could this be the day he has been waiting for? He approaches gently as both sense one another. The horse heads to the exit just before the rancher closes the corral. Both breathe heavily. The rancher smiles and turns away, leaving the gate open.

Months pass and the rancher wonders if he'll ever see the wild mustang again. And then one day, the rancher finds the wild mustang running laps in his corral. The rancher enters the corral and closes the gate behind him.

For a long time, I felt like the wild mustang. In my own eyes, I was everything I needed to be. I tried to fill the void in my life with material things. But what I really needed was to end the struggle and learn how to be more than a simple consumer. *I needed something greater to which I could surrender myself.*

Looking back now, I can see how huge and all-consuming my struggle to keep everyone happy, to please, and to perform was. I'm over it. Although this season has been overwhelming, I've been set free from all of those struggles. I'm learning what true freedom is: living a simple life, enjoying simple activities, and most importantly, *learning to live in the present.*

As I embrace silence and solitude, I'm learning about myself—the lost, but now found, Gracie.

My Thoughts & Notes

_____
_____
_____
_____
_____
_____
_____
_____
_____
_____
_____
_____
_____

The Forgiveness Factor

Whoever said, "To err is human; to forgive, divine" was absolutely right, because forgiveness often requires an effort that seems superhuman. But, at its root, *forgiveness is all about you*. In order to forgive, you must be completely self-aware. You must learn to forgive yourself in order to forgive others. It's one of the hardest things to learn, and to practice.

All of us make mistakes and hurt others. Unfortunately, that's just part of life. But one of the truest marks of someone's character is how they handle those mistakes and those hurts that they cause. We may often demand immediate apologies from those who have wronged us, but are we so quick to offer the apologies when we have wronged others?

Imagine that you've been made an incredible offer. A wealthy benefactor has offered to buy up all of your debt: student loans, medical bills, mortgage. He'll buy up all of your debt and forgive it *on one condition*: that you forgive every debt that anyone has ever owed you that you forgive everyone who has ever done you wrong.

The possibilities would be endless. Imagine what you could do without any debts holding you down! And all you'd have to do is *forgive*. Could you do that? Write a list of everyone you've been resenting, everyone who owes you money, and everyone who's broken your heart. *What would you say to them?* How would you rebuild a bridge that burned down long ago?

But if you could do it, if you could forgive, you would know a freedom like no other. You could cast off the chains that bind you to your old hurts and your old debts. *It would be like a rebirth.*

It often seems that we live in self-made bubbles and interact with only a handful of people who already agree with us. But our common humanity unites us all. We should be kind to one another. We should love one another and help one another in times of need.

Why is it that we have no problem volunteering and donating money, yet we have the hardest time forgiving those who have hurt us? Maybe you've heard the analogy: Continuing to resent someone, refusing to forgive them, is like drinking poison and expecting it to kill the other person. In reality, we are only hurting ourselves.

Break the chains that bind you to your past heartbreaks. Tear up the deed on a debt you are holding. Forgive someone today, and you'll find that you are really forgiving yourself.

My Thoughts & Notes

Walking the Camino Part 1

Here in the US, the word "pilgrims" makes us think of Thanksgiving: of tall-hatted English people and Native Americans, sitting together along a wooden table. When I first learned about pilgrims at five or six years old, I never dreamed that someday, I would be one too.

The Pilgrims of American history put their trust in God and crossed the Atlantic Ocean. But Christian pilgrims have been making trips, or *pilgrimages*, to ancient Biblical sites for centuries. At first, pilgrims went to locations like Jerusalem, longing to walk the streets that Jesus had walked. Later, people began to make pilgrimages to the burial places of saints, like the Vatican and the *Catedral de Santiago de Compostela* in Spain, a cathedral where St. James is buried.

Since the 9th century AD, pilgrims have walked along a web of paths, the *"Camino de Santiago"* ("The Way of St. James") to the cathedral, bringing questions that only God can answer. *So what made me leave my comfortable home and risk everything to walk the Camino?* The story of my pilgrimage begins at the ending of my marriage.

The end of my marriage came out of nowhere and shattered my life. My best friend, my husband, decided one day to call it quits. He said he was "tired" of being married to me and "needed to live his life." *I thought we had everything:* the right cars, the right jobs, the second home in the mountains. Our kids graduated from Christian schools and went to college on the East Coast. On the outside, we had the perfect life. On the inside—that was another story.

In this dark season, I grew deeper in my faith. I realized that only God could heal my wounds. I had become so addicted to status and possessions that I had forgotten who I was. God had brought all of my idols down around me to show me what was real. I lost some friends and sold some things I didn't need. I found my purpose: helping others.

My journey of faith brought me to *Spiritual Direction*, a course of theological study. As I studied, my fascination with St. Ignatius led me to the *Camino de Santiago*. The traditions, symbols, and routes to Santiago have lasted for centuries, and I was drawn to the tradition of bringing questions to have answered along the pilgrimage. Would God answer my questions too?

Almost before I knew what was happening, I booked a walking tour of the *Camino de Santiago*. I was committed. I would make a pilgrimage, and God would answer all my questions. I made arrangements to leave my family (which now included a newborn grandson), my business, my friends, and my home for a month and travel the Camino alone. There was no turning back now.

My Thoughts & Notes

_____

_____

_____

_____

_____

_____

_____

_____

_____

_____

Walking the Camino Part 2

As I flew to France to begin my Camino journey, my heart began to race. I saw my life in images passing before my eyes: my daughter's face, my son's wedding day, my grandson's face. I felt a sudden surge of panic. As the flight attendant read off her list of safety instructions, I remembered that I had come here to learn and to trust God. I prayed—*God, please lead me where you want me to go and bring me home*—and fell asleep.

I woke up in France, alone and tired, with only my high-school French skills to depend on. Although I'd been overseas before, I had never traveled alone. For the next 30 days, I would be completely on my own. I missed my family. I took a bus and a train to St. Jean Pied de Port, the starting place for my Camino pilgrimage. I'd been advised to take a few days to get acclimated to the time and altitude change, but I wanted to get started. So I set off on my pilgrimage the next morning at sunrise with a 20-mile walk.

The day was cloudy with a light drizzle as I started on my journey. I felt surprisingly good considering the eleven-hour flight I'd just taken. A beautiful French woman pointed towards a marker—a yellow arrow. It was my first sign. Scattered along the path, these yellow arrows are the only thing keeping pilgrims going in the right direction.

On my first day, I walked through treacherous terrain at a 5,000-foot elevation. People die on the Camino, and most deaths happen within the first few days due to falling rocks and steep cliffs. As I approached Roncesvalles, my legs shook and my feet ached. It took all my will to move each foot in turn. After I checked into my hotel, I made the first adjustment to my pilgrimage: I bought a red 12-speed mountain bike that I named "Ruby." Encouraged at the thought of traveling by bike the next day, I sank into a deep and grateful sleep.

At breakfast the next morning, a gentleman named Fernando asked if I was a pilgrim. I would hear that question many times over the next month. I told him I was and that I would be riding my bike to Pamplona. He looked at my ordinary shorts and blouse, and his face turned serious. "Well, you're going to need these." He reached into his bag and pulled out a pair of biking shorts. I was speechless. I'd heard that the Spanish people were generous, but I hadn't expected that level of giving.

I declined and reassured Fernando that I would be fine. He warned me that I would need better equipment just to survive, let alone finish. I said goodbye to Fernando and took off. As I started the day's uphill ride, I realized what he had meant. The paths went from narrow, gravelly passes to rough roads filled with rocks and boulders. It was the longest day of my life.

Finally, I neared Pamplona. Tears were running down my face. I felt so stupid. I couldn't finish. It was too hard. As I pushed my bike up a hill too steep to ride, I kept repeating: *I can do all things through Christ who strengthens me.* Suddenly, I felt a rush of energy wash over me, and I began to sing and to praise God. I wouldn't be going home the next day. I'd be going to Estella.

My Thoughts & Notes

_____

_____

_____

_____

_____

_____

Walking the Camino Part 3

On my third day, I woke up feeling pretty good. I wanted to get an early start on my planned 40-mile journey for the day, but God had other plans: my bike had a flat tire. After some help from a few fellow pilgrims or "Camino Angels" as they are sometimes called, I was on my way to Estella.

As I left Pamplona, I found myself in a residential neighborhood without a fellow pilgrim in sight. I was lost. By the grace of God, a kind woman and her daughter came out of their house to tell me that I was about 4 kilometers off course and that I needed to head back the way I came. They offered me a glass of cold water and sliced watermelon. I accepted gladly, and we began talking.

The women told me they had both been born and raised in Pamplona, yet had never done the Camino. They were shocked to hear I was traveling alone, and called me *valiente*—brave. Encouraged by their kind words, I thanked them profusely and continued on my way towards Pie de Perdon - a steep mountain range. I prayed to God every second of the way, asking for forgiveness and begging for mercy. As I approached the summit, I could hear a group of younger adults laughing and sharing in the beauty all around. For that moment, everything was good.

As I made my final approach to Estella, I encountered my second Camino angel. I was following a well-paved road when I heard a car horn behind me. I pulled over to the side of the road and a small pickup truck pulled up alongside me. "THIS IS AN ON-RAMP FOR A MAJOR HIGHWAY! TURN AROUND NOW!" Before I could turn around to say thank you, the truck was gone. My angel was out of sight.

I pulled into Estella during a holiday celebration. People lined the streets, dressed in white and red and singing. I could feel the strong sense of community. Seeing families eating, laughing, and celebrating together reminded me of my family, and all of the holidays and milestones we'd spent together. Seeing those families gave me hope that I would finish this pilgrimage and return home to make more memories.

On the Camino, you meet people from all walks of life. Three young men, friends riding the Camino for sport, nicknamed me *"Graciela la Machina"* because of my riding endurance. Over the next few days, they asked me about my faith and challenged my perspective. The last time I saw them, they asked me to pray for them. My heart was filled with joy and I knew this was true fulfillment.

Another person that God brought to my path was Leonardo, a 70-year-old man wearing a skirt and heavy eye makeup. I knew God wanted me to approach him, so I gently introduced myself and we began talking. I told him about my purpose for walking the Camino, my family, faith, and background. Leonardo shared with me a story of childhood sexual abuse and spoke of his unbearable shame about it.

We sat for two hours, talking, weeping, and holding each other. Leonardo had gone on to study pharmacy, and had eventually married. He had been faithful for 52 years until the death of his wife five years prior. We prayed together and he called me his Camino angel. I will never forget Leonardo.

My Thoughts & Notes

_____

_____

_____

_____

_____

Walking the Camino Part 4

As I finally approached my destination, the *Catedral de Santiago de Compostela*, I felt as filled with anticipation and excitement as a mother about to give birth. Before entering the cathedral, I felt the need to reach out to a few people to make amends. Jesus once told a man bringing an offering to leave it behind and go make things right with his brother. Maybe there's a lesson there: *we should make sure our relationships are in good standing before we ask for blessings for ourselves.*

In keeping with Camino tradition, I brought a rock from home to leave in the Compostela. Leaving the rock symbolizes leaving behind your burdens and celebrating the freedom that comes from forgiveness. As I approached the Compostela, I was shocked by how commercialized it looked. It was loud and touristy, a sharp contrast from the peace I had so often felt during the pilgrimage. But the contrast reminded me that *God lives in us. Not in buildings, but in our souls.*

On the Camino, I felt God tugging at my heart the entire time, reminding me to trust in Him. I imagined that's how Peter must have felt when God asked him, *"Do you love me?"* And, like Peter, I always responded, *Of course I trust you, Father!* But God wants to see physical actions as well as words. *I need to truly live the practice of trusting God first.* That was the Camino's greatest lesson for me.

I brought three questions with me on my pilgrimage:

1. *Am I supposed to become a full-time missionary?*

2. *Will I ever remarry or have a life partner?*

3. *God, would you consider giving me a glimpse of the next chapter of my life?*

My first question was answered on the second day. I was on my bike when God said, *Gracie, in my eyes you're already a full-time missionary. You help the poor, pray for the sick, and run a business which helps change lives. Continue to witness and to teach My word. I need you to be where you are.*

My second question was answered about a week into my pilgrimage. Since I was traveling alone, I ate most meals by myself. I went to bed early and didn't socialize. I spent the majority of my time in silence. I felt God ask me, *How's that solitude working out?* I realized that I missed laughing. I missed companionship. I was thankful that my heart was not hardened enough to want solitude.

My third question was answered two days before the end of my journey. I felt God chuckle at me and say, *Gracie, don't worry about yesterday. Don't worry about tomorrow. Focus on today. Be here. Be in the now.* I felt God lift my anxiety away in a single breath. I kept repeating: *Be here, be in the now.*

For many years, I was lost. I allowed others to determine my direction instead of following the arrows God had set out for me. My pilgrimage changed me from the inside out. I am committed to paying attention to the arrows in my path, and to helping others along the Camino of life.

My Thoughts & Notes

_____

_____

_____

_____

_____

Day 11

Why I Started My Own Business Part 1

I will always remember the phone call from my sister Lupe that changed my life forever. Lupe was talking so fast that I didn't understand a word until I heard, "She's going to refuse treatment." *Our mother was refusing treatment for her cancer.*

My mother had never smoked a day in her life and rarely drank, yet she was diagnosed with stage-four lung cancer. But with her faith and toughness, she somehow took the news in stride. She was confident in her decision.

I felt my heart fall into my stomach. All I wanted to do was cry and call my sister Lucy. But I couldn't; Lucy had already been dead for nine months. Her four-year battle with ovarian cancer withered not only her body, but also the spirits of our whole family. *How could we face this again?* I knew I would have to be there for my father.

My professional life was completely different from my home life. My investment banking career was taking off, and my family was starting to enjoy the benefits. We'd just come back from our second trip to Maui in twelve months. Our kids were in private schools and, for the first time in a long time, we had more than enough. *Yet, for the first time, my life felt empty.* Even though I was working so hard, I still had a deep need to make a difference.

My mother's courage gave me strength I'd never known before. At the pinnacle of my investment banking career, I resigned and never looked back. I reached out to some of my contacts, and soon The Grace Group was providing fundraising services to its first client. Now I could make my own schedule. Now I could spend time with my mother in her last days.

Humans are hardwired to feel a connection to people and things we love or care about. Sometimes we suppress these feelings through the fear of what others will think. And we create prisons using the opposite of connection: isolation from society, from each other. Even though my life looked like a mansion from the outside, on the inside it was a prison. I created a prison for myself because I wanted to look good for other people. *Are you living in a prison you created?*

I needed a way out. And somehow, my mother's death gave me new life. She rescued me from a desert that would have sucked every bit of my soul dry.

My Thoughts & Notes

_____

_____

_____

_____

_____

_____

_____

_____

_____

_____

_____

_____

_____

_____

Why I Started My Own Business Part 2

Being an entrepreneur is like trying to plug eleven holes in a dam with your ten fingers. We're problem solvers. We look at the impossible as just another challenge; that's what wakes us up in the morning. And we know that sometimes it takes years to see the final results of your actions: I'm motivated by the idea that Neil Armstrong took fragments of the Wright Brothers' plane to the moon with him. We build on the visions of those who came before us.

I built The Grace Group because I believed excellence could be offered as a service. I knew fundraising consultants were a dime a dozen, so I decided to be different. I gave smaller organizations the same attention and expertise usually only available to top-tier nonprofits. For every one of my clients, major donor gifts and private family foundation giving both increased. My clients began to believe in themselves. *I had become a broker of hope.*

Are you feeling the urge, deep down inside, to start your own business too? Maybe you feel it when you talk about the dreams you once had. Use that feeling to begin again, to cast a new vision for your life. *What would it look like to live your dream?*

Use these feelings to create an outlet for your passion. God created every person in His image, yet still unique. You have a spark of that divine creativity too.

It's important to surround yourself with people who support your passion. Since most people aren't living their dreams yet, you'll probably have to look around a bit to find your encouragers.

When you're a new entrepreneur just starting out, support from a loved one or mentor can make all the difference. They'll help you learn from their mistakes so you can make your own. Be open to what life brings you; your next mentor might even be someone who's in your life right now.

As The Grace Group began to grow, my mentors encouraged me to spend as much time with my mother as possible. I began praying for clients as I would for my family and friends. I asked my clients if there was anything I could pray about with them. At first, some clients were shocked, but everyone learned to love this question. Eventually, every one of my clients was praying with me before our meetings.

The freedom to be your own boss can be seen as a luxury, but it's really a tremendous responsibility. I use the golden rule as the basis of my work ethic. How would I like to be treated? Would I want an email response the same day? Would I want a handwritten thank-you note? This is how good entrepreneurs should handle themselves. We must set the bar higher, not lower ourselves to it.

Sometimes, new life comes through death. What would you change if you had a second chance at life?

My Thoughts & Notes

_____

_____

_____

_____

_____

_____

_____

_____

_____

The Beauty of Transitions Part 1

Sailors say you don't know the integrity of a ship's hull until it's weathered a few storms. Transitions in life are like storms at sea; they test the integrity of our character. Sometimes life is sunshine at the beach, and other times it's a hurricane that destroys everything you've ever owned and makes you question your every belief. It's during these times of transition that we learn what we're made of.

Back in 1988, I was working with a small team at Focus on The Family to launch some Hispanic initiatives. We were syndicating Dr. Dobson's show in new markets and the test results were off the charts. In cities like Los Angeles, Miami, San Antonio, and New York, Focus on The Family's traditional views resonated with Hispanic radio listeners. Since I'd grown up with devout Mexican Catholic parents, I felt I knew what would work with this audience.

After some time working on special projects, my colleagues at Focus on The Family let me know that I was on track to become the first woman on the development team. Peb Jackson, the head of the team, had made quite a name for himself at the organization. His charismatic demeanor was amazing; his ability to connect with people was something I really admired. He was always genuine and left you with a smile.

Before meeting Peb and his team, I'd always thought of fundraising in terms of senior citizens mailing in five-dollar checks to causes they found through churches or social clubs. What I learned there opened my eyes. Everyone worked together and brought new ideas to the table. Peb sometimes talked about donors like they were his extended family. Graduation cards, baby announcements, and wedding invitations from donors covered his desk.

During one of our meetings, the development team laid out the fundraising events for the upcoming year. There were men's fishing events, a golf tournament, a men's weekend retreat, an event at a baseball game, a men's Bible retreat, and a men's breakfast series.

"Do you have any events designed for women?" I asked the group. It was not my intention to call anyone out; I'd always been treated like an equal member of the team. But the fact that I was the first woman ever to serve on the development team explained the lack of fundraising events targeting women.

The room went silent. "Grace, what did you have in mind?" Peb asked.

Four and a half months later I was coordinating the first ever Focus on The Family Women's Retreat in Palm Springs, California. We arranged everything, from preparing tea and snacks for the fifty women as they arrived from the airport to sending their luggage ahead of them to the hotel. After a private tour of the offices and a small welcoming reception with Dr. & Mrs. Dobson, we loaded two charter buses and took off for the desert.

My Thoughts & Notes

_____

_____

_____

_____

_____

_____

_____

_____

_____

The Beauty of Transitions Part 2

On the drive out to the first-ever Focus on the Family Women's Retreat in Palm Springs, I ran through my checklist over a hundred times. Things were running too smoothly; I had to have forgotten something. Judging by the laughter in the background, people were having fun. But all I could think of was everything that could go wrong.

Soon, the ladies pulled up to the hotel to be greeted by my team members. Each woman received a small bag containing sunscreen, a water bottle, a retreat program, and an invitation to attend a fashion show. One of our attendees had a new clothing line, and we'd be showing her work to end the retreat.

Mrs. Dobson was our keynote speaker, and she brought along some of the speakers she was touring with. After her speech, I heard someone say, "Grace, you can breathe. I think we made it!" Our attendees were calling this the most inspiring weekend they'd ever had. I smiled to myself, thinking how scared I'd been on the ride out. But I still had a nervous feeling in my stomach, and I knew it wouldn't go away until after the fashion show.

"Three, two, one, go, go, go!" someone yelled from behind the stage. One by one our fashion models, all conference attendees, walked out to music and a cheering crowd. I looked around and saw everything in slow motion. The ladies were cheering for one another, clapping in unison and singing along. I knew at that moment that we had created something special. We had found a new group of donors, and we had given these ladies a sense of community once only experienced by their husbands.

As the models filed back out, the emcee addressed the crowd. It was time for the grand finale. There was no turning back now. "Ladies, we have one more surprise for you," the emcee continued. "Yesterday, at the pool, a couple of French models on vacation asked if they could participate in this fashion show, and we said yes!"

From behind the stage, I held my breath as I watched the "French models" walk out from behind the curtain. Laughter, applause, and loud whistles rocked the room. Our French models were really the three male members of our development team, doing their best runway walk complete with heels and makeup.

A few hours later, as I was loading my car to head back, Peb found me in the parking lot. I froze, nervous. "You know, Grace, we've just raised the amount that our last five events for men brought in…combined!" I thought he was joking!

"Do you think my wife will see the pictures from the show?" Peb asked with a grin.

I exhaled with relief. "I'll make sure of it."

I'll never forget that drive home. That was the day I realized that I'd need to get over my fear of failure at some point. The fear I'd put myself through all weekend was far worse than actually failing could ever have been.

My Thoughts & Notes

_____

_____

_____

_____

_____

_____

_____

The Sanchez Family Part 1

Life is risky, especially these days. We drive cars while talking on our phones, applying makeup, and singing along with the radio. But risk can also enrich our lives—by pushing us out of our comfort zone to confront our worst fears. The story of my parents demonstrates the value of taking a risk and betting everything on a dream.

My father Rodolfo "Rudy" Sanchez was born in Leon, Guanajuato, about a hundred miles northeast of Guadalajara in the middle of Mexico. He moved with his family to Chihuahua, then settled in the border town of Juarez. There, he worked as a rancher and was responsible for mending fences for the property manager. Rudy was a hard worker and gained responsibility quickly because of his attitude and work ethic. He was often the first one to arrive and the last one to leave.

My mother was born and raised in Chihuahua and moved to Juarez when she was a teenager. My mother knew almost nothing of her history because she was an orphan. She had an identical twin sister with whom she reunited with after almost 30 years of separation, and most of their family history was recalled through stories and secondhand accounts.

My mother's greatest insecurity was never knowing her family or why they abandoned her. I can only imagine the pain associated with growing up in an orphanage in Mexico. People often described my mother as reserved, serious, or closed off. These personality traits are usually associated with damaged people who don't want others getting too close. But behind my mother's stern facade, she only wanted her children to live a better life than hers.

My mother was tough and bright. She was always planning something or working on a new idea. She had an entrepreneurial spirit and knew how to make a buck. I remember her telling me stories about selling homemade breakfast burritos to construction workers on her way to work. She used the money to buy us new clothes, better food, or something else for the family; she rarely spent money on herself. That was her nature.

During and after World War II, agricultural laborers were in short supply around the country—but especially in western states. My father was an experienced farmer working mostly in Texas at the time. He later joined a federally-run program that brought laborers from Mexico to states like California, Arizona, and Nevada. After a few years, he was able to find work for both himself and my mother at a fruit cannery in Central California. The workers' living quarters were cramped and packed with children. The days were long and arduous. In a leap of courage, they left Central California for Los Angeles.

My parents settled in Compton, California. It was the 1950s. James Dean, Elvis, and Marlon Brando were running Hollywood. Los Angeles had a soaring middle class, a baby boom, and Chicanos in zoot suits with chains riding in big, shiny cars. Los Angeles, the city Jack Kerouac called "a jungle," had become home.

My Thoughts & Notes

_____

_____

_____

_____

_____

_____

_____

The Sanchez Family Part 2

My mother had 5 children in 9 years. My father worked at an oil refinery near Long Beach and my mother stayed at home with those five kids. I was number six.

At just 29 years old, my mother believed she was too old to have another baby. When I was born, my oldest sister was just starting high school. Other siblings were in junior high and grade school; my youngest brother was only just out of diapers. My mother was ready to be done with babies. She was way too busy to take pictures, so you won't see many baby pictures of me.

My sister Lucy liked to carry me around and tell people I was her baby. My mother was absolutely mortified to think that people might believe one of her daughters was an unwed teenage mother. I believe this is why Lucy and I were so close; she gave me the love and affection I needed as an infant, and I gave her something she could call her own.

As the last of six children, I enjoyed a life very different from that of my oldest sister. She spent her first years surrounded by strangers in a cannery in northern California, while I spent mine surrounded by family. I was the only child in the family to attend private school, since the public schools in Compton were already in decline by the early 1970s. My family was established, my brothers and sisters were dating—but there I was, little Gracie, keeping my mother in a phase of life she so badly wanted to leave.

One day, my father bought me a new bike. It seemed that I had been asking for one for an eternity, but really, it was probably only a few months. The neighborhood kids rode around on shiny new bikes with streamers on the handlebars. Meanwhile, I rode around on an old hand-me-down that had probably belonged to all of my brothers and sisters in turn.

I remember opening up the garage to see my shiny, glitter-painted new bike with white tires and pink streamers on the handlebars. In my hurry to rush my new bike out of the garage, I heard a terrible noise. The end of my handlebar scraped my father's new car, leaving behind a long scratch just beneath the passenger's door handle. I rushed out the door, hearing my mother and father yelling in Spanish to one another.

As I rode down the street, I imagined I could feel envious looks from the neighborhood kids. I felt truly free, with the wind in my hair and California sun warming my face. My heart was content. I never wanted to go back, because I knew I'd be in trouble when I got home. I imagined riding my bike all the way to the beach. It was the perfect place to start over, and I would be able to ride my bike every day.

Much later, I learned that I was the first person in my family to get a new bike. I was too young to understand how envious my siblings were that day. My brothers used to joke about getting new bikes every year. But it wasn't until I was in high school that I realized why my brother kept a lock cutter under his bed.

My Thoughts & Notes

_____

_____

_____

_____

_____

_____

_____

The Sanchez Family Part 3

When I was growing up, life was simple. We kids kept our mother busy, and my father worked long days. During weekends and vacations, we traveled in our station wagon to places like Seattle, Yellowstone, El Paso, Alberta (in Canada), and many parts of Mexico. We camped often because we never stayed in hotels.

My father would load up the station wagon, strap a mattress to the roof, and cram us all into the car. I remember singing songs in Spanish with my mother about life in Chihuahua and Mexico. We'd listen to mariachi music and my father would explain the lyrics to us. I learned a lot from my culture's music, from these songs filled with fervor and passion. Hearing these songs still fills me with pride today.

I never understood how my father decided where we would go; I was convinced he just threw darts at a map. Have you ever driven from Los Angeles to Canada with six kids in a car and a mattress on the roof? It was unconventional, but it was family time, and we always managed to make it interesting.

Once, we were somewhere in Utah on our way to Yellowstone National Park. My father thought we could drive straight through to Wyoming, but after the long drive, we were a car full of irritable people. My father felt the tension in the air and began looking for a place to stop for the night. He saw lights on a hill and a lawn that looked like the entrance to a large park. He didn't want to pay the overnight camping fee, so he stopped where he saw two picnic tables near a tree.

In the dark, we unloaded the car and leaned both picnic tables against one another. We threw a sheet over the tables to make a tent and slid the mattress in between. Some of us slept in the car while my older brothers slept under the stars in their Army & Navy Surplus Store sleeping bags. It wasn't fancy but it was cheap. I fell asleep thinking about the breakfast my mother would make in the morning. It was usually eggs and chorizo burritos with homemade salsa from a mason jar, along with Tang to drink.

Just after daybreak, I woke up to a loud knock on the window of the car. I screamed as I saw two large uniformed men peeking into the car asking if anyone was awake. My father poked his head out of the makeshift tent. In his broken English, he complimented the campgrounds and told the men, whom he assumed were park rangers, that he'd be out quickly. I think he even invited them to stay for breakfast.

My sisters and brothers translated for my parents. I still remember the look on my father's face when he realized what had happened. My mother was mortified and began frantically cleaning up the campsite. The mattress was thrown back on the car, and we left before making breakfast. My brother and I complained that we were hungry, but everyone else in the car was silent.

About fifteen minutes later, my father erupted into laughter. He was laughing so hard he was wiping tears from his eyes. My mother tried to be mad but couldn't help joining the hilarity. My brothers and sisters started to laugh, but I didn't understand why at first.

Later, I found out the truth about our impromptu camping trip. The lighted city on the hill was a maximum-security prison. The lawn leading up to the entrance was a waiting area families could use when picking up loved ones. When the prison guards asked if he was waiting for someone, my father grandly complimented the "park rangers" on the beautiful park grounds - while wearing only his tighty whities.

My Thoughts & Notes

_____

_____

The Power of Hope

Have you ever seen a little plant growing in the crevices of a sidewalk? It seems impossible that such a small thing as a sprout has the strength to crack apart roads, the symbols of human skill and speed, but there they are. Those persistent little sprouts always make me think of hope, and how powerful it is. Like those sprouts, hope is a bright spot of color in a gray world, reminding us that there's more to life than the daily grind of work.

Do you feel like you're struggling these days, friend? The seemingly endless churn of bad news lately has a lot of people feeling down. Together with our own local troubles, we hear reports of every disaster for miles around. That can really take its toll. And as we've seen recently, even the rich, successful, and beautiful aren't immune to feeling lost and hopeless.

Lately, I've been doing some writing and revisiting about a pretty rough time in my life. After my first marriage ended, I felt utterly hopeless, as though I'd failed at my most important job. My parents were still married. In fact, they stayed married until one of them passed—until death they did part, the way it's supposed to go. How could I, who had been given so many advantages, so many gifts, fail where they had succeeded?

I felt utterly humiliated, hollowed out, as though I couldn't go on. I can't tell you what might have become of me if not for the love and grace of my family and friends, who reminded me that where there is life, there is hope. I learned to seize that hope and to go on, sometimes one day at a time, sometimes one minute at a time, until I could once again see a future and a new life for myself.

I want to remind you that it's okay to take care of yourself. Of course, you have obligations: work, school, family. But it's vital for you to recharge and renew your own spirit. Even if it's just a few extra minutes in the morning, or at night before bed, to *say a quick prayer or affirmation*, it will make a big difference. *Eat as regularly and as well* as you can manage, and drink plenty of water. Try to remember to *breathe slowly and deeply*, since breathing quickly can make feelings of worry and anxiety worse.

I can't promise you that things will turn out the way you want them. I can't tell you that the lost loved one will return, that your heart will un-break, that you will be restored as you were. But I can tell you that there is beauty in the brokenness of life. And I can tell you some of my story here in these pages, so that you will see how God, in his wisdom and faithfulness, has made the joy and beauty I now enjoy in my life from the ashes of my past sorrows.

And, most importantly, I ask you to cultivate hope. Like that little sprout pushing through a sidewalk or street, hope will reappear and remind you that there is still so much to love in this old world. The sun will always rise. The seasons will always change. People will always be their good, bad, lying, truthful, gloriously messy and complicated selves. With hope in our hearts, we can build a new world, a new future, together.

My Thoughts & Notes

_____

_____

_____

_____

_____

_____

_____

_____

Launching My New Life Part 1

The car took the exit before Sepulveda and began to loop around towards a separate parking lot. I was used to a very different experience when flying out of LAX. *People fly in private planes all the time,* I kept telling myself. *No reason to be so nervous.* But all I could think about was how a little girl from Compton made it here.

"You've got one bag, right?" the driver asked as I heard the pop of the trunk.

"Yes, sir. Just a carry-on." He smiled and ran around to get the door. I reached into my purse to grab some cash. I wanted to give the driver a generous tip so he would think I was used to this lifestyle. I held out a wad of cash and the driver politely whispered, "It's okay, ma'am, it's been taken care of by Mr. Tichenor." You have a wonderful trip." I insisted, and after an awkward shuffle, he took the money. I asked for my bag, and the driver chuckled. "It's been loaded. It'll be waiting for you in Dallas."

I remember thinking that the level of trust granted to millionaires was extraordinary. No security lines, no baggage scans or TSA agents. Our captain poked his head out of the door. "We've been cleared to take off behind the next regional. Are you all set?" I had forgotten we were already 20 minutes late because of an accident on the 605. "Yes. And I'm so sorry I'm late." I hurried up the stairs, took one last look at the early morning sky, and smiled.

As I sat down, it all began to sink in: *I was the only passenger on this jet.* To the pilots and flight attendant, I must have looked like a little kid in a candy shop, swiveling my head around to see everything. I felt the plane jolt once as it started towards the runway, and with one left turn we were moving forward fast. Before I knew it, we were airborne and banking south over Palos Verdes. Golden sunbeams danced over the foothills. My face was glued to the window as we climbed into the clouds and away from the sprawl of Los Angeles.

Once we hit cruising altitude, one of the pilots came into the cabin and sat beside a small wooden table set perfectly with neatly placed napkins and coasters. "Looks like we'll make up the time in the air. Might even be a little early. We'll pick up Mr. Tichenor and prepare lunch in Dallas, then start making our way to M-E-X." Deep in thought, I broke my gaze out the window and responded, "Sounds good." Then I dove back into my fading memory of how I had met the man whose jet this was—the man we were *en route* to pick up.

My Thoughts & Notes

Launching My New Life Part 2

Mac—MacHenry Tichenor, Sr.—was standing outside his car, looking up at the plane as it glided down the runway. In just a few minutes, he was sitting across from me, asking rapid-fire questions about work, my family, and when lunch was going to be served. It was good to see him.

"Gracie, you know I told Carlos, if he would just understand that Mexico wants a football team, we could get to the next step." I looked up and nodded. "So that's what we're going to do on this trip." He could tell I was a little confused. "We're going to make him make us have to prove it."

I was always amazed at how Mac took an enormously complicated process and made it sound as easy as boiling water. He'd probably say it's because he was a Texan. Whatever the reason, I found the simplicity reassuring. I remembered how I'd met Mac so many years ago.

It was 1989 when I first spoke to Mac. He was Chairman of the Board at Tichenor Media Systems in Dallas, Texas, and I was a mother of two working for Focus on The Family in Pomona, California. Tichenor Media Systems had just purchased a conglomerate of Latino-focused radio stations. His name had stuck out in the article because he, seemingly at random, had recently donated $10,000 to Focus on The Family with a personal check.

The first time I spoke with Mac, I thanked him for his recent gift. I was in my twenties, a new fundraiser at Focus on The Family with big ideas and tons of ambition. I was working on a new project: bringing Focus's message to the Latino community. This was uncharted territory for Focus, and many saw it as risky, steering away from what was working well.

So you might say I had an ulterior motive when I called Mac to thank him. I saw an opportunity to speak with someone who could verify my belief that radio was the medium that would best reach my people.

That first day, when I called Mac to thank him for his donation to Focus on The Family, I was nervous. After a few minutes, he asked me why I had really called. His question was so sincere that I had to tell him the truth. I wanted to talk to him about radio, specifically Latino radio.

Our initial conversation lasted over an hour. Mac knew the statistics and the marketplace like the back of his hand. He had access to the fastest-growing demographic in the country. I told him Focus on The Family wanted to do a version of Dr. Dobson's hit radio show in Spanish. Before we ended our call, he told me he wanted in. He put me back through to his assistant so I could overnight our demo tapes to him. That was the start of a relationship and mentorship that would span across two marriages, four bosses, and countless lessons learned.

My Thoughts & Notes

_____

_____

_____

_____

_____

_____

_____

_____

_____

Gracie's Secret Part 1

I heard the school bathroom door close. I held my breath to listen for anyone else in the room. *I was alone.* My knees were pulled so tightly to my chest that I could feel my heartbeat on my thighs. I tried to take a deep breath, but it felt like someone was holding my head underwater. Finally, I managed a sigh, a big inhale and exhale.

My hands loosened their grip on my knees and my head tilted upward as I tried to hold back my tears. It was almost time for class, and I'd have to go in and act as if nothing was wrong. My mind raced feverishly, almost as if I were planning a heist or prison break. Talking to myself just above a whisper, I said, *"If you act perfect, nobody will see any difference."*

The first day of school used to be my favorite day of the year—until the sexual abuse began. School had been something I always enjoyed. I felt safe at school. I enjoyed working in groups, and like any other kid, I looked forward to recess the most. But all that changed during the summer before I entered the 4th grade.

My mother grew up as an orphan, never having known her own parents. I know she must have longed for the comfort of belonging to a family. She just wanted to give us the normalcy of having grandparents to spend time with. After all, we humans we are hard-wired to build connections to other people. Those connections form the basis for our social behavior. But what happens when people betray that trust?

My parents had befriended an older couple in the neighborhood and had encouraged us to accept them as our "grandparents." What my mother didn't know was that she was leading me into the den of a vicious monster, a man who stole my innocence and imprisoned me in my own body with guilt, shame, and insecurity. My struggle to overcome the pain and fear caused by someone whom my family had trusted would take a terrible toll on me later in life.

I took a deep breath and unlocked the door. As I dried my tears, I smiled in the mirror. *At least pretend to be happy,* I told myself. Many animals were able to hide in plain sight, so why couldn't I?

I made a deal with the devil that day that would cost me nearly everything I loved. It wasn't until decades later that I was able to tear down the walls I built around my pain and truly learn to love and forgive myself.

My Thoughts & Notes

Gracie's Secret Part 2

I walked into Mrs. Holloway's classroom and gave her a big hug. Maybe I held on a little too long. Mrs. Holloway knelt down and looked into my eyes. "Gracie, I'm so happy to have you in my classroom this year."

For one perfect moment, my heart felt complete. I smiled at Mrs. Holloway and took my seat near the back of the room. Before I sat down, I asked another boy in my class if I could switch seats with him to sit closer to the board. "Gracie, that's not your assigned seat," Mrs. Holloway said.

"But my eyes hurt if I have to squint to see."

Mrs. Holloway tilted her head. "Okay, that's fine," she said. "Let's get going, everyone." I scurried to the front of the class, took my seat, and folded my hands over my new notebook. "Everyone starts today with an A in my class. It's up to you to keep it," Mrs. Holloway called out as she wrote out the daily agenda and date on the chalkboard.

This would be my job from now on. My overactive brain devised a plan as I began to sweat, worrying that Mrs. Holloway would ask my parents if they'd had my eyes tested. I needed to keep that A average, go to a good school like really smart people did, become a doctor or something very successful, and make money. Lots and lots of money.

I threw myself into school. I was good at school. I loved being the only person in my class to get perfect test scores. I always wrote more pages than required for every assigned paper. My parents would hang my tests on the fridge and brag to their friends. My mother would say, "Do you believe she was hit by a car, thrown 50 feet, and hit her head on a curb? She almost died. I prayed to God to let her live a normal life. Now look, she is an A student!" My father would walk by and rub the top of my head and say, "My little smart girl."

Mrs. Holloway must have realized something was wrong, but I never told her my terrible secret. I wanted to so badly, but I was afraid she would think badly of me if she knew. And I believed my parents would be upset if I told Mrs. Holloway. But Mrs. Holloway showed me real, unconditional love. Throughout the year, she would send notes home complimenting my parents. And every day, I fought to become what I was pretending to be.

I began to feel I needed affirmation to perform, which drove me to overcompensate. I couldn't relate to my classmates because I felt they could tell I was hiding something. I wore being called a "teacher's pet" like a badge of honor. Instead of playing outside, I asked Mrs. Holloway if I could help with classroom tasks during recess and lunch. I lived for praise, slowly becoming addicted to the rush I got whenever I received a compliment.

My Thoughts & Notes

Gracie's Secret Part 3

My abuse continued for almost four years, right up until my abuser's sudden death.

My abuser always told me not to tell anyone. He said he would tell my parents, tell the school, get me in trouble. He asked me what my parents would think if they found out. He made it sound like I had done something wrong.

Worst of all, he'd remind me of the hardships my parents endured to become American citizens. Something like this, he said, would mean our whole family would be sent back to Mexico. I remember trying to scream, but no sound would come out—just a dry rattle.

When my parents would leave to visit family in El Paso, I would cry and come up with every excuse I could think of not to spend the night at my abuser's house. My mother would yell, *"They love you! You're going to hurt their feelings!"* I wished for a way to really hurt him.

My abuser died of a heart attack and everyone wept for his sudden, tragic death. I wanted to believe my prayers killed him. I cried too, but my tears of joy turned painful when I realized I would never see him being arrested or beaten up by my older brothers. I wanted to tell everyone the truth at last, but I was afraid they would think it was my fault or that I was making it up for attention. So I buried my feelings and built a wall around my pain.

I kept up my façade through middle school and into high school. I was committed to graduating top of the class as the valedictorian. But I didn't stop there. I was class representative, Treasurer, and then ASB President. I was a cheerleader and also started working at 15. I was earning money, making straight A's, and applying to colleges so I could get a business degree. I saw pictures in magazines of powerful ladies in suits holding meetings, and I believed that was the definition of success. I knew no one would question a strong woman.

One day in my junior year, I became very ill, vomiting uncontrollably. But I couldn't think about going to the doctor: I was cramming for my final exam in honors chemistry. My grade had fluctuated between A- and B+ all semester long. Anything less than an A would destroy my valedictorian dreams. I pushed through the pain and studied through the night.

After the chemistry test, I saw a doctor who diagnosed a bleeding ulcer. I was seventeen. "Are you under any stress?" he asked. "Just your normal school stress," I responded. The doctor told me to slow down a little after I rattled off a dozen clubs and projects I was participating in just that semester. "You're going to blow a gasket going at that speed. You're young; enjoy these times. You'll never get them back." I couldn't wait to prove this doctor wrong.

In my mind, I had everything figured out. I was filled with rage. I would devour anything that came into my path. My drive was a deadly cocktail of insecurities, anger, pain, and fear. I knew my family wanted a smart and successful daughter, not a damaged, sexually abused embarrassment. It was my duty as the youngest to surpass my siblings. Anything less, even telling the truth, was unthinkable.

Sexual abuse happens more frequently than we'd like to think. According to the National Center for Victims of Crime, 1 in 5 women and 1 in 20 men are victims of sexual abuse, with children being most vulnerable between the ages of 7 and 13. Sexual abuse can lead to lower self-esteem, distorted views of sex, and even suicide.

I wish I could have given my younger self this advice: if this has happened to you, you must talk to someone. Don't do what I did and convince yourself that you can hide the truth forever. Only after years of working through my past could I tear down the wall I placed in front of my darkest secret. I could have avoided years of grief by speaking up.

My Thoughts & Notes

The Importance of Being Mindful

It's not easy to be mindful these days. Between the demands of work and family, it can feel as if we're being pulled in a lot of different directions. How can we help relieve that overstretched feeling and unwind a bit? I believe *mindfulness* is the key.

What does it mean to be mindful? Basically, it just means being aware of where you are at each moment in time. To be mindful means that wherever you are, whatever you're doing, you're doing it consciously and without judgment. Being mindful can help you reduce feelings of anxiety so you can enjoy your life a little more.

So how do we get to this mindful state? It can be as easy as paying attention to your breathing. When we're busy and rushing around, we often take quick, slow breaths. This can cause us to feel more anxious. To relax and practice mindfulness wherever you are, try taking some deep, slow breaths. Slow down your thinking and notice where you are and what's around you. Concentrate on each deep, slow breath and feel yourself relaxing.

When you're trying to be more mindful, it helps to *use as many of your senses as you can.* Look around you and notice small details. Are there flowers in the trees? Can you see different colors in the room? Make sure to keep up your slow, deep breaths as you take in the sights surrounding you. While you're breathing in, be aware of all the smells you experience. Don't analyze what you see or smell; just take it in and be fully present where you are.

Take some time to truly feel your body. You can do a mini-scan of your body, noticing any sensations you experience. Are you sitting on metal bleachers at a child's soccer practice? On soft cushions at home? Are you feeling a breeze on your face, or the pressure of your feet against the floor? Don't worry too much about each feeling, just note them and set them aside. Check in with each part of your body from your scalp all the way down to the bottom of your feet. Breathe deeply and slowly and be aware of your body and how it feels.

Listening can be part of mindfulness too. Mindfulness can mean *truly listening when others speak to you,* instead of rushing your mind ahead to what you'll say next. Breathe slowly and evenly. Listen and make eye contact. When you truly open yourself to hearing what people are saying, when you're present in yourself, you'll find yourself feeling deeper connections to the people around you.

By focusing on yourself, you can become more mindful. Even though you start out by concentrating on yourself and your senses, mindfulness also helps you to pay more attention to other people and how you relate to them. And when you practice mindfulness regularly, you can help yourself to feel more relaxed, more conscious of the world around you.

My Thoughts & Notes

_____

_____

_____

_____

_____

_____

_____

_____

The Covenant of Friendship Part 1

Friendship is truly one of life's greatest mysteries. Why do we place so much emphasis on our relationships? Humans naturally seek companionship. We love to share experiences with other people whom we feel close to.

If friendship is key to our happiness, isolation is its opposite. Our criminal justice system uses isolation as punishment: isolation from people, loved ones, and *friends*. Our society places so much importance in the idea of friendship that we even created a TV series called "Friends" about young people going through life together.

We usually don't have a choice in who our family members are, but sometimes we're lucky enough to have relatives who are both family and friends. And sometimes our friends become our chosen family, closer even than those who are related to us by blood. Unfortunately, the opposite can also be true: sometimes our family can act more like "halfway friends."

The Book of Ruth in the Old Testament is a wonderful story about the power of relationships, especially friendship. But Ruth's story begins with an all-too-human tragedy, a relocation due to a natural disaster.

Naomi, her husband, and her two sons were forced to leave Bethlehem for Moab because of a famine in her hometown. Even after having to leave behind her culture, extended family, and everything she had ever known, Naomi knew she had what she needed the most—her family. However, shortly after arriving at Moab, Naomi's husband suddenly died, leaving her and their sons behind.

I try to imagine how this must have devastated Naomi. I can only imagine having to flee my home with my family, only to face a terrible loss in an unfamiliar place. My heart goes out to Naomi; I'm sure she must have wanted to go back home. Even though Naomi knew she couldn't return, the love of her sons must have given her some peace of mind.

As the story continues, Naomi's two sons married women from Moab. To Naomi, this must have meant that Moab would truly be her new home. It also meant she would gain two new daughters, Ruth and Orpah.

Naomi greeted Ruth and Orpah with open arms, but this new family wasn't what she had envisioned. Not long afterwards, both of Naomi's sons died, and she was alone again, with only two daughters through marriage to keep her company.

Have you ever been in this situation: struggling in an unfamiliar place? Trying to keep your family together while reeling from devastating losses? These are the times when we find out who our true friends are. When things are good, we have plenty of friends. But when things get tough, friends get scarce. Why is that? Maybe it's because those were *halfway friends*, not *covenant partners*.

What's the difference between halfway friends and covenant partners? *Halfway friends* are quick to be there when times are good, but seem to disappear once the good times end. *Covenant partners* are there for you when times are good, and they draw even closer to you when times get bad.

After Naomi's sons died, she decided to take her daughters-in-law back to Bethlehem. It was a long journey, and she needed her daughters by her side if she hoped to make it home alive. Halfway to Bethlehem, Orpah decided to turn around and go back to Moab. But Ruth decided to stay and honor her mother-in-law, since she had made a covenant with her husband to be there for his family, even if he died.

Good friends—real covenant partners—don't run away during bad times. Not only do they not run away, they stay close and build one another up. Covenant partners call upon something bigger in order to bring hope to their suffering friends. Ruth reminded Naomi that God still had a plan for her, even though Naomi believed that God was punishing her through the death of her husband and sons.

Trust is vitally important in friendships, and especially so with covenant partners. In my darkest hours, my closest friends reached out to me. They never asked if I needed help; they just showed up. They shielded me when I was weak, and they reminded me that life would carry on. I trusted them and, in return, they trusted me.

Trust is the glue that binds friendships. Halfway friends don't see the benefit in earning trust because they are only focused on the short term. Covenant partners understand that trust is passed on through giving without needing to be recognized. That's acting like the Holy Spirit.

It takes a lot of self-confidence to be a covenant partner. Halfway friends are shallow people. They see unfortunate situations as a kind of competition in which they can look and feel better than their suffering friend. But covenant partners aren't concerned with surface appearances. They're confident in themselves. Covenant partners build one another up, rather than tear each other down.

When things get tough for one of your friends, are you a halfway friend who runs away or uses the situation to feel better about yourself? Or are you a covenant partner? I strive to be a covenant partner every day. I've learned the hard way that it's much better to kiss your Orpah goodbye.

My Thoughts & Notes

_____

_____

_____

_____

_____

_____

The Key to My Happiness

H*appiness*. It seems like the one universal desire in this crazy busy world. Multi-billion-dollar empires are built on promises that this makeup, this diet pill, this dress, will finally make you happy. But those promises are lies; eventually that new possession isn't enough, so you have to buy another, and another.

And honestly, I used to believe that too. When I was younger, I often felt that if I bought certain things, if I did what other people did, that I'd find the elusive secret to happiness. I tried so hard, for so many years, to live the way that happy people seemed to live. Somehow, no matter how hard I tried, I never seemed to get to happiness.

Why wasn't I as happy as everyone else? What was I doing wrong? It took me way too long to figure out the key to happiness, so I want to share it with you today.

The problem with finding happiness was that I was looking at everyone else rather than myself. I was spending so much time and effort looking at how others were living—what they were buying, what they were wearing—that I had forgotten to be me. Why should I copy what others do? Why should I live as they live? I had to learn to listen to myself, to love myself, to take care of myself first and best.

Once I stopped worrying about others' lives and how mine didn't measure up, I found that I could better appreciate all of the things I had. And I found that I didn't even need all of the things that I had. I've been letting go of so many possessions and so many attitudes that weren't making me feel better. Living more simply has shown me how much freedom there is in letting go of comparisons.

So here's the key to my happiness: *Share, don't compare.* Don't worry about how other people are living. Don't spend too much time staring at their smiling pictures on social media and making yourself feel bad because you think their life is so much better than yours.

Instead, share who you are and what you have with others. Share your story. Share your truth. Live as if your life were precious and wonderful and too good not to share—*because it is.*

I get it—sometimes it feels easier and more fun to complain about how difficult things are or about how we wish we lived somewhere else, had better possessions, or did a different job. But, even if we made all of those changes, we'd still be unhappy because we would be looking outside ourselves for happiness.

So there's the secret. You are already enough, right now, right where you are. You are already precious and wonderful and too good not to share. Get out there and ***live.***

My Thoughts & Notes

_____

_____

_____

_____

_____

_____

_____

_____

_____

_____

_____

_____

You Can't Buy Happiness

One of the mistakes we make when searching for happiness is to think that we can buy it in a store. Today, online shopping means that virtually anything you could ever want to own is a finger-tap or a mouse-click away. And with free shipping and 24-hour access, there's no stopping us from buying anything we want, any time we want.

Celebrities sell us the idea that we can find freedom and joy through buying cosmetics and diet drinks. Our friends all seem to be living much more vibrant and joyful lives across our social media feeds. So we try to keep up by buying the same things they have. All of this consumption can leave us *financially overextended* and *emotionally drained*.

Have you been throwing money at online retailers, hoping that the next new delivery will help you find happiness? If so, you might want to take a step back and make some important adjustments to help save your budget—and your emotional health.

- **Put a HALT on your shopping.** Do you find yourself shopping more when you're **h**ungry, **a**ngry, **l**onely, or **t**ired? These feelings can lead us to unwise decisions. If you are feeling one of these emotions, try another option for dealing with it: have a snack, take a rest, or call a friend.

- **No news is good news.** Do you get up-to-the-minute sale listings from online retailers? Unsubscribe from all of those email lists and push notifications so you won't be tempted by impulse buys.

- **Remove temptation.** Take shopping apps off your phone. That way you won't be tempted to look for deals "just in case." Ad blockers can help you avoid seeing targeted ads on social media.

- **Shop your closet first.** Is there something you've been wanting to buy? Look through what you have already. Chances are you already have one of those items or something pretty close to it. And if you have a lot of new or gently used clothes you don't want or never got around to returning, you can always sell them online or donate them to a nearby shelter or charity.

- **Take a step back.** Remember that you are not defined by your clothes or your possessions. You are enough already, right now, just the way you are. You don't need anyone else's approval.

Happiness isn't something you can get with your bank account. But you can still earn interest on it—by sharing it with others. When you spread happiness and love around to your friends (or to others through service and volunteering), you increase them more than you could ever imagine.

And when you feel more connected to a community that's bigger than you and your needs, you'll find you're much less worried about whether you're keeping up with the Joneses. You'll save money, sure, but you'll be saving yourself too.

My Thoughts & Notes

_____

_____

_____

_____

Opening My Home, Sharing My Life

What does home mean to you? To me, home is my happy place. My home is my haven of rest and place of peace. And yet, in 2017, I only spent 7 nights in my own house. How can both of those things be true? The answer is a story that starts in my childhood.

My mother always used a certain saying when she faced difficult times. The saying is rooted in my Mexican culture—*"Something good will come out of a negative situation."* She always believed that even bad circumstances could lead to something good. I could never have imagined back then that I'd someday have the opportunity to learn this for myself.

As a result of my divorce, I inherited a sizable tax bill. I was already reeling from the divorce, so receiving the bill was a bit overwhelming, to say the least. But I knew I had to be responsible and meet my obligations. So I set up a payment plan and figured that I'd just pay it off over time.

Back in 2014, I enrolled in a two-year Spiritual Direction program based in Santa Rosa. I was going to school every other Tuesday up in the Bay Area, which usually meant a Monday-Wednesday travel schedule. On a whim one week, I asked my assistant to research Airbnb and to list my house for the days that I'd be traveling.

Well, the rest is history—my house became very popular and I was booking up within hours of each listing. Encouraged by this success, I decided to go even further and to list my house during the times I was away visiting my children and clients on the East Coast. Within a few months, my house became a very hot commodity and I was booking up faster than ever.

My friends often say that I have the *gift of hospitality*. I've always enjoyed opening up my home to host parties and making people feel comfortable. I love to cook and host large family gatherings. I also enjoy hosting visiting professors or parents coming to nearby colleges to visit their children. As strange as it sounds, I view renting out my home through Airbnb as an extension of that hospitality—my way of welcoming others into my community.

In 2017, I rented out my house *357 days out of the year*. Yes, I slept 7 nights in my own house. Thanks to my Airbnb renters, I settled my tax bill and I've even built up a savings reserve. But, most importantly, I've met some incredible people who have stayed at my "Little Yellow House in the Village." I have to say that my mother was right—something very good came out of this negative situation.

Although my home is small, I think it's exceptionally cute and comfortable. I see my little yellow house as a beach cottage— just without the beach! It has an elegant simplicity about it. When I walk into my home, I feel a sense of love. Many of my guests say my home is very peaceful and that they feel my spirit there. It seems to me that they must feel the love, joy and peace that surround my home.

The front porch is a perfect spot to enjoy my morning coffee. My backyard is a little paradise with a waterfall and lots of tree coverage; it's a wonderful place to enjoy a glass of wine or some private meditation. My renovated kitchen is perfect for trying new recipes or dancing to salsa music with friends and family, and I always keep it clean and well-stocked for my guests.

I see my guests as *friends* rather than *strangers* and I believe this is why people book my house months—or even years—in advance. I've had several repeat visitors and have received many beautiful notes from guests saying how much they enjoyed their experience. Guests like to say that my little cottage is their "home away from home."

You might be surprised to hear that my neighbors have been very supportive of my Airbnb venture. They often compliment my guests, who are usually very friendly and respectful of our community. Some of my neighbors have even booked my home themselves to host their own family and friends. I love being able to help them keep their visiting loved ones close by!

If you're interested in listing with Airbnb yourself, it's a great idea to do a little something extra for your guests. I prepare welcome packages for my guests that include the names of local restaurants, coffee shops, and nearby points of interest for sightseeing. I also sometimes include a bottle of wine for my guests.

Here are a few more recommendations if you want to become an Airbnb host:

- Increase your home insurance policy.

- Store your valuables in a secure location.

- Maximize the unique attraction of your home. I'm near several colleges, which helps make my home a popular choice for my guests.

- Respond quickly to your guests' inquiries.

- Include some nice amenities like high quality shampoos and conditioners, a blow dryer, etc. I like to set out designer towels for an extra luxurious touch.

Even after hosting almost 200 guests through Airbnb, I still enjoy sharing my home with others. In fact, sharing my home has only deepened my love for it. It's fun to host people from all around the world: I've hosted guests from Brazil, Australia, China, India, Switzerland, and Israel. I like to think that hosting so many people has enriched my life as much as it has the lives of my guests.

My Thoughts & Notes

Balancing Work, Life, and Family Part 1

I was once asked, "Grace, how do you define success?" My answer was simple: *Success is not being able to tell the difference between work and play.*

Balancing your life and figuring out what to prioritize is an ongoing journey, yet I believe it all begins with this question: *What do you value the most?* I sometimes like to visualize "jars" that represent the various areas of my life: God/spiritual life, children, family, friends, work/career, finances, self-care, etc.

Thinking about my time and effort as things I can put in these jars helps me to be the best person I can be for my loved ones and the world. In order to assess how I spend my time and resources, I evaluate two items at the end of the month: my calendar and my checkbook. They show me how much time I'm spending with my children and loved ones in contrast to how I'm spending my financial resources.

I try to live my life while keeping the end of that life in my mind. Of course, I don't mean that in a morbid way, but in terms of thinking about the legacy I want to leave when I go. For instance, sometimes I imagine myself at my funeral. What would people say about me? Would they talk about what a great fundraiser I was, or about how I raised millions of dollars for charities? Or would they talk about my character?

I want people to say that I was a kind and generous person. I would like my friends to say that I was a good friend, that I took time to make fun memories and walk in fellowship with them. I would like my children to say that I was a loving and attentive mother who took time to attend their baseball games and taught them values and morals. I hope my staff members at <u>The Grace Group</u> will say that I was a leader who led by example with integrity and excellence. I have made it my life's goal to be worthy of these words when my time on earth comes to an end.

As time passes, I wonder: is it possible that women have been tricked to believe that we could "have it all" when we know, deep down, that this isn't the goal we should have? It's challenging to be a top executive, an attentive wife, a good and loving mother, *and* a well-rounded person, since we all only have the same 24 hours in a day. What we need to do is to establish what we value most. Then, maybe instead of focusing on *having it all*, we can think more about *being it all*.

For the past 15 years, at the beginning of the year, I have written a personal mission statement where I ask myself: *Who do I want to BE in the world this year?* I use this as a road map for the year ahead. What kind of mother do I want to BE? What type of leader/ boss do I want to BE? What kind of friend do I want to BE? These questions serve as my internal accountability system in determining what projects or opportunities I take on.

My Thoughts & Notes

_____

_____

_____

_____

_____

_____

_____

_____

_____

Balancing Work, Life, and Family Part 2

As I evaluate how I use my time and my resources, I determine priorities based on *roles that only I can fill.* For example, if I have a client meeting in the evening and my daughter needs me to be at a mother/daughter event at the same time; I can always send a staff member to the client meeting. But I'm the only person who can be my daughter's mom, so being with her takes priority.

I was a single mother for several years while raising my two sons. I realized that it was going to be important for me to have special time with them, so meals together were a priority. My mother always made home-cooked meals for our family, and I wanted to offer my sons the same tradition. Thankfully, I had a full-time nanny who assisted with picking them up from school, which made life a little easier for us all.

I later remarried and had my daughter while I continued to work full-time. Our nanny remained with us, and having a husband to help carry the load was a blessing. Finding enough time to nourish my marriage, participate in my children's activities, and care for my baby was not easy, but balancing it all became my mission. Family dinners together were a must. We all sat together and enjoyed home-cooked meals—the slow cooker became my best friend.

At the dinner table, we talked about our days and used our time together to instill values and what my children refer to as "Mama's life lessons." I worked for World Vision for 7 years while my children were younger, and I am grateful to have had the privilege of working from home. I had the heavy responsibility of raising $1 million each year from my donors. That wasn't easy, but I managed to meet and exceed my yearly goals while attending my children's school events and still being a good wife, daughter, sister, and friend. It was more important for me to be a good wife and mother than a top producer at work. Yet I believe that, because I chose wisely, I was also able to experience success in my career.

Once I became an entrepreneur, I had the freedom to set my own schedule and work at my own pace. I worked long hours, but I always made time to be there for my children—and family dinners remained a top priority. I woke up an hour early each day to allow myself 30 minutes of quiet time for prayer and meditation. I also squeezed in a 30-minute workout so I could maintain a sense of wellness. I found that making my children's school lunches the night before was a good way to get a jump start on the day. I embraced time management skills that helped me make the best use of my time.

As a business owner, it was up to me to deliver excellent customer service without compromising my family values in the process. As the years passed, I built a strong team of staff members who embraced our culture of excellence and who helped carry the workload. This allowed me the flexibility to prioritize my faith and family. I have always encouraged my staff members to put family first, and I want to lead by example.

I believe in the saying "From she to whom much has been given, much will be required." In my business, I strive to put *people above profit*. I want my staff to feel valued and supported, rather than pushed to limits that strain their personal well-being.

My Thoughts & Notes

_____

_____

_____

_____

_____

_____

Balancing Work, Life, and Family Part 3

During this season of my life, I don't have to worry as much about young kids or the typical stresses of life. But I still have to balance my work responsibilities and my passions.

Although my business is demanding in terms of sales and leadership, I have more freedom with my time, so traveling to see my children and grandchildren is a priority. I balance my love life and time with my friends with my travels around the world. In addition, I have <u>Spiritual Direction</u> clients that I usually see in the evenings or on the weekends. I enjoy writing my weekly blog posts too, so I have to plan time to write, exercise, meet with my family, and see my friends. I am a learner at heart, so in my free time, I like to read or listen to podcasts. As I get older, I find myself praying, "Lord, teach me to number my days that I may grow in wisdom."

I encourage you to take time to figure out what you value most. That will help you determine how you will spend your time and resources. And be sure to carve time out for self-care, since we usually end up at the bottom of the list. We all tend to give so much of ourselves to our spouses, children, loved ones and careers, so we sometimes start to feel run down or depressed, like we're running on an endless hamster wheel.

Not balancing our work and private time has real consequences for our health and relationships. When you're tired and overburdened your body, mind and spirit will suffer in the process. Always stressed? Stress weakens our immune system and can worsen the symptoms from any medical condition. And if you're working too much, you might miss important family events or milestones. This can leave you feeling resentful and left out. Here are a few suggestions to help you start or maintain balance:

- **Create a list of your top priorities**. Put family events on the calendar and keep a daily to-do list at home and work. Having a plan helps maintain focus.

- **Manage your time wisely.** Cut out or delegate activities you can't handle. Organize your errands or chores so you do a little every day; don't save all the laundry for your day off. Do only what needs to be done and let the rest go.

- **"No" is a complete sentence.** Whether it's a co-worker asking you to take on an extra project or your child's teacher asking you to organize the class party, remember that *it's okay to respectfully say no.*

- **Leave work at work.** With so much access to technology, you may need to set limits on taking work home or answering emails after hours.

Unfortunately, we can't manufacture time. We all get only 24 hours a day, so it's critical to set boundaries with work so we have time for the activities and relationships we enjoy. Once you figure out your balance between work and life, you'll find you're more able to be productive and happy both at work and at home.

My Thoughts & Notes

_____

_____

_____

_____

_____

_____

_____

Embracing the Season of Gratitude

Fall has arrived with its cooler weather and gently tumbling leaves. Everywhere you look, you're reminded of the upcoming holiday season. It's almost Thanksgiving, a time for celebrating family and gratitude. But what if you don't exactly feel like celebrating those things? Maybe you've had a difficult year, with a job loss, a divorce, or some other tough circumstance. Maybe you have a hard time dealing with family members or in-laws. Or maybe you just always find yourself feeling a little down around this time of year and you're not sure why.

The good news is: you're not alone. A lot of people feel anxious and down around the holidays, whether they've had a tough year or not. Sometimes we get caught up in our ideas of what a "perfect" holiday should be like. Whether that means a holiday just like the ones you knew as a child, or the exact opposite of the ones in your past, it's a lot of pressure to put on yourself.

Remember that the past is done, and that even the holidays that seem perfect in your memories weren't really that way. The best holiday experience is one that you can manage and feel good about at the end. Sometimes that means doing less, and that's okay! Your family and friends would rather have you feeling relaxed and able to enjoy yourself than stressed out and running around trying to make everything perfect.

Are you hosting a holiday gathering this year? It's perfectly fine to ask your guests to bring dishes. Or you might want to consider pre-making (or even pre-ordering) some of the food for the gathering. Enlist the kids (or kids at heart!) in your life to help make fun decorations for your home and table. A shortcut here and there won't make much difference to the day, and can help you be more present and have more fun.

Are you worried about not getting along with one or more people who will be present? Think about things that might happen and how you can handle them constructively. If you'll be at someone else's home, you can prepare plans to take a break or even leave if things get difficult. If you're hosting, consider enlisting help: friends or other relatives who can help steer the conversation to safer ground, or who can help defuse problems that arise.

One thing that can help set the tone for a happy holiday occasion is to keep gratitude at the center of your celebration. Ask each person at the table to mention something they're grateful for. Even if it's been a rough year, chances are that everyone can think of one good thing that they're thankful for. You might also consider working some sort of charitable help or volunteer experience into your holiday celebration. What better way to keep gratitude on everyone's mind than to share what they have, whether it's time or money, with those who need encouragement and help?

Remember, the holidays are supposed to be a positive time. Even if you are struggling with some difficult circumstances, you have a lot to celebrate and to be thankful for. Putting gratitude and love at the center of your season will help you to have a happier holiday—and will improve the rest of your year too.

My Thoughts & Notes

_____

_____

_____

_____

_____

_____

_____

_____

Managing Holidays When Relationships Are Complicated Part 1

Most of us have beloved holiday traditions that we celebrated with our families, and that we plan to share with our own families one day. Passing on foods and celebrations helps us build our own family traditions. These traditions shape us and help us to define ourselves and our families.

But what happens when our future doesn't turn out the way we'd hoped it would? After a painful breakup, it can be hard to reconcile your happy holiday wishes with the reality of your situation. But for your own sake and the sake of your children (if children are involved), it's important to figure out a set of holiday traditions and routines that works for you.

My own life changed dramatically when my first marriage ended and I was left on my own with two young sons. I had to deal with the pain and anxiety of my divorce while keeping up day-to-day routines for the boys. Holidays presented a new challenge: how could I honor both sides of the family? How could I make sure that the boys got to experience everything they were used to? And what would become of my holiday traditions?

As I reflect upon those years when my sons were younger and I had to manage sharing the holidays with their father, my ex-husband, I'm glad to say that I always made the boys my first and foremost priority. Co-parenting requires strong communication skills and a lot of respectful planning ahead. I found that allowing plenty of time to discuss plans helped us to find satisfactory solutions with a lot less stress.

My sons' father and I often alternated our large holidays. During the time we were married, Christmas, Easter, Thanksgiving, and birthdays had been big occasions for our shared family. But eventually, we managed to reach an agreement to alternate the big holidays each year. This helped us minimize what could have been hectic schedules for the children.

Later, I remarried and had a daughter. Unfortunately, my second marriage also ended in divorce, which added more complexity to our holiday situation. However, as a result of good communication with my daughter's father, we could often reach an agreement to keep things peaceful so that our daughter would not experience trauma or stress.

During the first few years after my second divorce, my daughter's father allowed me to take our daughter to the East Coast so that she and I could celebrate with my sons. This was very important to me, because I felt my daughter really needed time with her older brothers. I remain grateful to my daughter's father for his kindness and consideration for us all.

Now that my sons are adults with wives and families of their own, sharing and joining events seems to be easier for everyone. It has been said that time heals all wounds. In this case, I would agree that time has allowed for any differences that I have had with my ex-husbands to heal and for us to grow as parents and as individuals.

My exes and I continue to encourage family gatherings and extend invitations to each other. I truly believe that this has enriched our lives and the lives of our children, and that it's helped deepen our children's connection as siblings. I have concluded that although we are not a traditional family, we are family.

My Thoughts & Notes

_____

_____

_____

_____

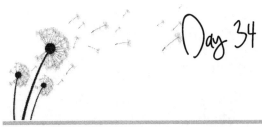

Managing Holidays When Relationships Are Complicated Part 2

Traditions have been very important throughout my life, especially when I was raising my children. I work hard to remain consistent in much of my holiday planning. This has always helped create a peaceful environment in my home, even during times when my relationships were difficult.

Cooking is one of my favorite hobbies, so I get very excited when the holidays come around. That's because some of my most cherished traditions involve food. My favorite holiday foods for Thanksgiving are creamed corn, baked yams and my homemade pumpkin pies. I believe that cooking is truly a labor of love that results in beautiful memories as we sit around the table and break bread together. When we cook for someone, it shows them how much we care about them, and sharing food strengthens community and family bonds.

To a child of Mexican heritage like me, Christmas always means tamales. Tamales are a food and a tradition in one, since preparing them requires several hours of cooking, working closely as a group. These days, I love to make tamales with my sister, daughter and nieces. All year long, I look forward to tamale-making time. We get to work together, laugh together, and, best of all, enjoy the final product—homemade tamales.

I also enjoy baking for the holidays, a tradition I have kept up for over 20 years. I love making a special Christmas cake for all of my neighbors every year. I especially look forward to delivering the cakes and seeing their smiling faces as they greet me at their door.

As strange as it may sound, I extend invitations to my exes when all the children are in town. I'm not sure if it is age or wisdom, but as I have grown older, I see family as the foundation of my life. One of the challenges for children of divorce is time—the time that is shared between homes. Because of this, I feel that I should do whatever I can to help make this challenge a little easier for everyone.

In conclusion, I would say that keeping things simple makes it easier for everyone to get along. The holidays are a stressful time, especially if you are co-parenting or have blended families. It's important to keep things as positive as possible and to hope that our children will not experience the painful effects that divorce or divided families can bring.

Sometimes, we can be way too hard on ourselves, especially if we feel like we have failed in a relationship. I believe it's important for us to be kind to ourselves and to others in this process. Try to put things in perspective. *Broken relationships do not define you.* Take time to reflect on all the good that the relationship brought into your life. Remind yourself of all of the blessings in your life, such as your health, your friendships, your family, and even your resilience and the ability to start over.

Most importantly, be kind to yourself. Take time to ask: *How do you want your holidays to look? What memories would you like to create? How would you like your children to remember the holidays?* If you decide to take a break from your traditions this year, allow yourself that freedom. If you'd like to start a new tradition, give yourself the freedom and grace to do so.

My Thoughts & Notes

_____

_____

_____

_____

_____

_____

Some Encouragement If You've Had a Tough Year

It's natural, as we reach the end of the year, to want to look back and celebrate accomplishments. But what if you feel like there isn't anything to celebrate? What if you feel like everyone else is doing great things while you're stuck in a rut? That's where a few of my friends find themselves this year, and I want to share with you what I shared with them.

Every day you are changing and every day you are growing. It may not feel that way, and it may seem strange to think of "growing" now that you're an adult, but you are. Every day you are becoming stronger and wiser, more your truest self. Have you learned some new things? Have you cared for your body and soul? Have you done your best to love your friends and family? *Those are excellent things to celebrate.*

It's easy to feel like we don't measure up when we compare ourselves to others. But remember, what you see on social media isn't always someone's reality. It's easy to apply filters, to leave out details, to shove anything you don't want anyone else to see just out of the frame of the camera. Resist the temptation to spend too much money just to impress others. Don't pretend to be someone you're not. You don't have to pretend or lie about yourself. *You are valuable just as you are.*

We've become too focused these days on productivity, on material things. What truly feeds our souls, what brings meaning to our lives, is not productivity but *community*. Reaching out to others, connecting to them, really talking to each other: those are the things that move us. Sharing a meal, opening up to others in conversation—these are real, doable things that *build bridges.*

Making these connections to others helps us to shed the self-doubt that holds us back. Then we can focus on developing our gifts more fully. Too often, others can see and appreciate our gifts better than we can. Give yourself the freedom to make big plans, to dream big dreams, or even to learn to be satisfied with yourself, right where you are. *When you learn to see yourself through others' eyes, it can help you to judge yourself less harshly.*

We're building a community here too, and I hope you'll grow along with us in the New Year. Even though we may not be able to change some of the big things that are going on in the world, each of us can work to make our corner of the world a little brighter. And it all starts with *loving yourself,* with being as gentle to yourself as you would be to a friend who's hurting. Love yourself and care for yourself first and best, and you may find you have the strength and the will to start making the changes you want to see in yourself—and in the world.

My Thoughts & Notes

_____

_____

_____

_____

_____

_____

_____

_____

_____

_____

Day 36

The Importance of Kindness

These days, I feel like the world could really use more kindness. Looking around outside, I can't help but notice that it seems to be in pretty short supply. But why does kindness matter? What does it mean to be kind? Kindness is one of the greatest gifts we've been given, and it's up to us to keep it going.

One of the most important things to realize about kindness is that *it can only be expressed by someone who's experienced it.* Kindness is something that's passed on. It's something that has to be learned—and taught. *And kindness can be as simple as you want it to be.* It's not only found in grand gestures and expensive gifts. It's found in the little things, like making eye contact and smiling when you're talking to the person making your coffee or ringing up your groceries. Help people remember that they're important, that they deserve respect and courtesy.

Being kind isn't just a matter of helping someone who asks for it. It's much more than that. Being kind is also about imagining yourself as another person, anticipating their needs, and offering help before it's asked for. After my first divorce, when I was distraught over the breakup of my marriage and overwhelmed by the reality of having to raise two small children on my own, I was touched by the many kindnesses that my friends and family showed me. Their kindness and love helped me to see that I could get through the tough time that I was having. I've never forgotten that, and now I try to bring kindness to others when they're in difficult situations too.

Bringing kindness to others is a wonderful thing to do. But we can't be kind to others if we aren't kind to ourselves. When I tell my daughter to be kind, I mean to herself first and foremost. It's no good trying to extend kindness, grace, and mercy to those around us if we are unable or unwilling, to extend that same grace and kindness to ourselves first.

It's easy sometimes to get caught up in our daily struggles and to forget that we are all struggling. All of us are flawed, imperfect people living in a flawed, imperfect world. But we've been given the amazing gifts of love and empathy to help us reach out to each other. And, most importantly, we've been given the ability to be kind—to ourselves and to those around us.

If you want to see more kindness, it's important to realize that it all begins with us. We have the power to tilt the balance of life in a positive direction. We may not be able to have everything we want in life, but we can always do something to make someone's day brighter. *Practice kindness. Show the kindness you want to see in the world.* Even if the kindness you show someone isn't returned, you still haven't lost a thing.

My Thoughts & Notes

_____

_____

_____

_____

_____

_____

_____

_____

_____

_____

The Holiday Traditions Part 1

The holidays are just around the corner and the days are getting shorter, so I've been doing a lot of thinking about *traditions*. Every family seems to have their own set of holiday traditions. Some of them have been around for generations, and some of them are newer, created by each individual family and shaped by their own experiences. Now that I'm a mother and grandmother, I love to think back to all of the traditions that were the mainstays of my childhood.

I was raised in a Catholic family, which usually included midnight mass on Christmas Eve. This may not be familiar to some of you, so I'll share a little more about this tradition. We would eat dinner around 7 in the evening and play games or watch Christmas movies. Even though we had a lot of fun doing that, going to mass at 11 was a must.

When we returned from the church service, we would all open up our Christmas gifts. I realize it might sound strange to keep young children up so late. But we loved the anticipation of opening up our Christmas gifts after mass! We got to do this because of our good behavior and our willingness to attend mass together as a family.

Another tradition in the Mexican culture is *"Las Posadas." Las Posadas* is a walking journey done in a group that re-enacts Mary and Joseph's journey. People walk through neighborhoods singing Christmas songs in Spanish as they announce that Jesus is about to be born. It's a wonderful community-wide celebration that helps spread Christmas cheer.

I was exposed to other wonderful Mexican Christmas traditions as a child. My favorite of all is the tradition of making tamales for our Christmas Eve dinner. I remember vividly the planning and preparation it took for us to come together to make the tamales. It entailed shopping, preparing the meat, and making the tamales as a family. From preparing the corn husks to rolling the meat filling into its corn dough base, tamale-making helped to make our family closer.

It is often said that cooking is a labor of love, and that is definitely true about making tamales. The part I enjoyed the most was sitting around the table with my siblings and my parents as we talked and joked and enjoyed being together. The reward of eating our homemade tamales at Christmas Eve dinner was just the icing on the cake. Our tamale tradition has followed me through most of my adult life, and now my sister and I join other women in my family to prepare tamales for our families at Christmas.

What are some of *your* favorite family traditions? Are they things you did while growing up or did you start them yourself for your own family?

I've been doing some thinking and talking about holiday traditions lately, and revisiting the traditions of my childhood. We all have different ways of celebrating our holidays, and it's interesting to see how those celebrations change when we have our own families!

When my children were younger, I began a tradition that we still carry out today. I would buy everyone matching pajamas and place them on their bed on Christmas Eve. That way, we could all wake up on Christmas Day wearing our new pajamas. In our family, Christmas morning has been our very special time together. It starts off with breakfast and opening up Christmas gifts; we take it slow and stay in our pajamas for most of the day. Our Christmas Day dinner is usually homemade tacos, which are a family favorite.

As the years have passed and my children have become adults, I have tried very hard to continue the tradition of making tamales and having the family together on Christmas Eve so that we can all enjoy Christmas Day. Christmas Eve usually includes our extended family: siblings, spouses, nieces, nephews. The count is often up to 30 or more people! It's fun to see how all the children enjoy each other's company. And I love that we can all eat our tamales and make beautiful memories together.

Now that our family has grown in number, we usually just buy gifts for the children. Instead of worrying about what to buy each other, the adults can simply sit and enjoy seeing the smiles on the little ones as they open up their gifts. It's so wonderful to see how the family grows and changes over the years, and it's a great time to make priceless memories.

One of the beauties of traditions is that we can carry on old ones from our childhood while still having the freedom to create new traditions. This tradition has faded over the years because my older children live on the East Coast, but we always used to go to a play or a theater show a few weeks before Christmas. However, I do still enjoy going to the movies on Christmas Day with my children. I realize that it's not very creative, but there is something so enjoyable about going to an afternoon movie with my now-adult children. I must confess that I have not always chosen the best movies to watch, but that usually turns out to be a funny part of the day and a memory in its own right.

My heart's desire is that my grandchildren will carry on the tradition of tamale-making and family gatherings. I hope to instill in them the love of family and traditions, of food, fun and laughter.

I realize that distance is a challenge for a lot of families these days. But I am committed to bringing my children together as often as I can so that we can continue to share in the beautiful joy of dinners, game nights, and laughter. It might mean that we won't all get to have a happy dinner together on Christmas Day, but whenever we're all under the same roof; *it will still feel like Christmas.*

My Thoughts & Notes

_____

_____

_____

_____

_____

How to Be a Blessing to Others This Holiday

I've been talking and writing a lot about the holidays, because I've seen how much my friends and others are doing this season, and how they're sometimes a little hesitant to talk about the struggles they're having. After all, this is supposed to be the *season of joy*, the time when everyone is cheerful—at least according to all the smiling family photos and Christmas letters detailing lots of accomplishments that land in the mailbox every day.

But we can't all be joyful all of the time. And it's a real challenge sometimes when you're juggling work, family, laundry, cooking, and a million other little things that never seem to get done. Add holiday decorating, gift shopping, and the usual round of seasonal get-togethers to the mix, and it's no wonder that folks feel a little stressed.

So I propose that we think a little bit outside the gift box here. Let's think of how we can help each other out. *How can we bless each other this holiday season?* First of all, let's be more open about the struggles we're facing. Let's talk more about the things that make us feel *stressed* as well as the things that make us feel *blessed*. Sometimes, just talking about our burdens make them feel lighter. And if we open up to our friends, we might just find that the things and the abilities we have can balance out the places where they need a little help.

Be sure to *check in* with your friends. Are there areas where you can pool your resources and get more done together? For example, my family loves making tamales for the holidays, but if you don't have a big family around you it can be a huge undertaking. So why not see if you can all get together and make tamales, or pies, or whatever holiday foods or crafts you need? Not only will the work go faster when more hands are involved, but you'll have a chance to catch up with each other, laugh a little, and feel that stress level drop for a while.

Even if you can't physically get together with your friends to make things, checking in via phone or text will give you and your friends a chance to bounce ideas around, recommend recipes or techniques, or just encourage each other.

If you're on the other side of this issue, if you find yourself feeling lonely and adrift during the holidays, then you have a wonderful gift to bring: *yourself*. If you have friends who could use a little help getting ready for the holiday, open up to them too. They may have wanted to involve you but weren't sure how to approach you.

Volunteering can be a great way to reach out to others during the holidays too, if you don't have local friends who need a hand. And when you open up to being a blessing, you may be pleasantly surprised to find yourself feeling a little of that holiday joy you've been hearing about. In this season and beyond, let's commit to reaching out and forming new memories and deeper connections.

My Thoughts & Notes

_____

_____

_____

_____

_____

_____

_____

_____

_____

When it Feels Like No One's Noticing You

This time of year, we're all feeling a little run down. And sometimes you just want someone to *notice*, to care, to ask how you're doing. I get it. I feel that way too sometimes! It's easy to feel discouraged when it seems like nobody notices all of the hard work you do every day. The whirl and pressure of the holidays can really bring those feelings out in a big way. But here's the good news: *you are seen. And you are loved.*

These days, this world can seem pretty dark. But here's something very important I want you to know: every time we do something good, no matter how small, it makes a little spark of light. It fixes some broken part of the world and makes it shine again. If we all remember this, if we all make one tiny spark at a time, each in our own way, the light we create will shine forth and bring us all joy.

We often tend to downplay the importance of what we do. How often have you heard someone say "Oh, I don't do anything really important, I just—" and then follow it with something like "I teach first grade," "I work at a call center," "I stay at home with my kids." How many times have we said that about our own jobs, our own deeds? Each of those paths is terribly important. None of those paths is better or more valuable than the others. Each of them can bring more knowledge, relief, comfort, or joy into this world. Sometimes we don't even realize the lives we touch each day, the light we bring just by giving someone a smile or a kind word.

I hope it helps you to hear that you are important. You matter, and the things you do matter. A friend of mine tells the story of a quote someone wrote in her high-school yearbook: *"If you do something beautiful and nobody notices, don't worry. When the sun comes up, half the world is asleep."* That really made me think! I've remembered this quote ever since and I try to live it out every day in my life.

You are doing great things, right now, just where you are, even though you may not feel like you are. Nobody you know has to see the good things you do in order for those good things to bring value. But there *is* someone who always notices and values and loves you. I believe God is ever-present in our lives. He sees your good deeds, and He knows your heart.

But if you're not comfortable with that idea (and I understand that not everyone might be), perhaps it helps to think of a friend who's glad to walk with you in good times and bad. *Hello, friend. You are working so hard and you are doing so well. I believe in you. I see you and I notice you, and I know how important you are. Now go out there and shine your light.*

My Thoughts & Notes

_____

_____

_____

_____

_____

_____

_____

_____

_____

_____

_____

Rejoice, Don't Resolve

The year is winding to a close and it seems like everyone is making lists. Lists of the things they loved this year, lists of the things they hated this year. And most of all, everyone is making lists of *resolutions*. And it seems that every year, most of those lists end up tossed aside, gathering dust. Then new lists are made at the end of the year and it all starts again!

So here's an idea: *What if you just...don't make New Year's resolutions this year?* It's way too common to list a bunch of impossible things that you know, deep down, are too much to ask of yourself. "This year, I will lose 25 pounds, find the person of my dreams, get discovered in Hollywood, climb Mount Everest, and run 2 marathons!" How could ANYONE accomplish a huge list like that? Don't set yourself up to feel like a failure at the end of the year.

People love to talk about what's wrong with them, what needs changing. I want to suggest that we flip that script, and we focus on all the amazing things we did in the past year. *But Grace,* I hear you saying, *I didn't DO anything amazing this past year.* Well, I'm here to tell you that's not a fair thing to say. You did great in 2018, even if you can't see it.

Not every accomplishment has to be huge to be celebrated. Were you on time to work and appointments more often than not? Did you make some great memories with family and friends? Did you do some fun things just for yourself? Did you enjoy some delicious meals? And did you take care of yourself and your loved ones? These are all things that you can put on your list! I bet that if you think back over what you've done in the previous year, you can think of a lot of small accomplishments that add up to a lot of joy and satisfaction.

You wouldn't let your friends obsess over the little things they didn't get done in the past year, so you can, and should, give yourself that same love and courtesy. Even if you feel like all you did this past year was work and pay bills and eat, *that's something to celebrate too!* Life is tough, and sometimes it seems like all you can do is hang on. We don't admit that to each other enough—*everyone is fighting battles that nobody else knows about.* So be gentle with yourself and celebrate the spirit that keeps you going and keeps you out there, taking care of business every day.

Let's scrap the resolution list this year and make a *rejoicing list* instead. I think that'll make the end of the year a little merrier for everyone!

My Thoughts & Notes

_____
_____
_____
_____
_____
_____
_____
_____
_____
_____
_____
_____

Forgiving Yourself When Dreams Don't Come True

Did you have a dream, a goal, for this year that didn't happen? Maybe there was a big project you wanted to finish, or a personal goal you set that you fell short of. So you are probably feeling bad about the thing you didn't achieve or the numbers that weren't met. But this is all up to how you see it. You are the one who decides if you succeed or fail at a task. You decide what success or failure is when it comes to what you do in your life.

Here are some things to consider when you're thinking about what you feel are your failures of the year:

- *Was the thing that happened really a failure?* One of the things we most often criticize ourselves for is the breakup of a relationship. But that's not always fair to ourselves. Relationships can break up for all kinds of reasons, many of them out of your control. Sometimes people just aren't right for each other! If you've had a rough breakup this year, try to be gentle with yourself and remember that it isn't all your fault.

- *Did you set a goal that was too high or unattainable?* If you set higher goals than you can reasonably achieve, then it's only natural that you won't meet the goal. Did you set a goal of reading 100 books and now you know there's no way you'll get there? Maybe you should look back at how many books you've actually read over the past few years and set your new goal based on that. It's not a real challenge if you set impossible standards for yourself.

- *It's okay to fail.* This is a hard one to face for some people. Our society is so devoted to, and obsessed with, success that we sometimes forget its twin, failure. Without failures, there are no successes. People sometimes pretend that they've never failed at anything but that is actually a terrible thing! If you've never failed at anything that means you're not trying to grow and change and stretch your abilities. Failure is how we learn.

- *Is this how you would treat a friend?* Suppose a friend came to you, heartbroken over something they weren't able to achieve. Chances are you wouldn't laugh at them and call them stupid or worthless. Then why would you do that to yourself? Do for yourself what you would for your friend. Forgive yourself, love yourself, and give yourself a little room to feel your feelings and grieve over where you missed the mark. Then put that failure aside so that you can focus on the New Year and its new challenges.

Every day you are growing and changing, even if you don't notice it. It is absolutely okay to fail at something, to not be excellent at whatever you try the first time out. Try to approach each new challenge with the mindset that, whatever happens, you will learn and grow from the experience. That can help you stop beating yourself up about the things you try that don't succeed.

My Thoughts & Notes

_____

_____

_____

_____

_____

_____

GRACE SANCHEZ

AUTHOR • ENTREPRENEUR • SPEAKER
•SPIRITUAL DIRECTOR•

Grace is a compelling and engaging storyteller with a rich set of life experiences that she's ready to share with your group!

Keynote Topics
- Healthy Work and Life Balance
- Overcoming Abusive Relationships
- Recovering from Divorce & Other Setbacks
- Spiritual Director and Finding a Center
- Balancing Faith and Finances
- Fundraising for Nonprofit Institutions

For more information or to book for speaking contact:

www.finding-gracie.com
(213) 952-8097

Made in the USA
San Bernardino, CA
17 May 2019